YANKEE MAGAZINE'S
Great Weekend Getaways in New England

YANKEE MAGAZINE'S
Great Weekend Getaways in New England

Favorite Driving Tours from
Yankee's Editors

Some of the material in this book previously appeared, before revision, in *The Yankee Traveler* newsletter, *Yankee Magazine's Travel Guide to New England,* and *Yankee* Magazine.

Text design and map illustrations by Karen Savary
Cover photo by Kindra Clineff

Library of Congress Cataloging-in-Publication Data is available.

ISBN 0-7627-0367-9
Co-published by Yankee Publishing Inc. and The Globe Pequot Press. Distributed to the trade by The Globe Pequot Press. Produced by Yankee Publishing Inc.

Printed in Canada.

First Edition
2 4 6 8 10 9 7 5 3 1 softcover

Contents

Acknowledgments

MANY OF THE TOURS IN THIS BOOK ORIGINATED IN THE *Yankee Traveler* newsletter. I would like to thank Janice Brand for her vision and hard work as editor on *The Yankee Traveler.* Her good taste, discriminating eye, and extensive knowledge of New England are reflected in these driving tours. I would like to thank designer Karen Savary for her creativity and especially for her special touch of hand drawing the maps. Research editor Louise Clayton steadfastly updated all the tours, down to the tiniest details of hours and prices on more than 600 essentials. After a while I wondered what she looked like *without* a phone attached to her ear. Our production team Paul Belliveau, Dave Ziarnowski, Rachel Kipka, Lucille Rines, and Brian Jenkins handled this project as they always do — with accuracy, dispatch, and humor. Lida Stinchfield's copyediting skills are unrivaled, and we at Yankee Publishing thank our lucky stars that she's ours. Lida says she couldn't do it without the excellent help of proofreader Anna Larson.

I would like to thank the talented authors whose writing makes this book a good read. I could not have included all the wonderful tips included in the "What the Locals Know" feature without the generosity of *Yankee* Magazine readers and other locals who have shared their favorite places with us. A big thanks to my colleagues in the Travel Group here at Yankee Publishing — Carol Connare, associate editor, and Mel Allen, editorial director — who shouldered my responsibilities while I took time out to edit *Great Weekend Getaways*. Finally I would like to thank our publishing director, Jamie Trowbridge, for his unflagging encouragement on this book.

Polly Bannister
Senior Associate Editor

Introduction

WHEN I MOVED TO NEW ENGLAND 25 YEARS AGO, I longed to learn about the people and places that define this region. I hankered to hop in the car and explore, but I needed a road map to the icons as well as to the small towns and personalities that make the area unique. I wanted to be spontaneous, but I didn't want to keep getting lost. What I wanted was this book, written by people who know New England better than anyone else.

Here you will find everything you need to plan a successful adventure. Whether you live in the region or are visiting from another part of the country, you'll see that these carefully designed driving itineraries highlight the best we have to offer. For this book we've selected our all-time favorite tours from the pages of *The Yankee Traveler* newsletter, *Yankee Magazine's Travel Guide to New England,* and *Yankee.* In more than 60 years of writing about New England, we have covered nearly every inch of the region. Our conclusion is that you will not find a more beautiful, historic, interesting, and fun place to visit.

Our compact six states are ideal for weekend getaways and day trips. We know how difficult it is to make time in a busy schedule, but we encourage you not to limit your travel to just a week's vacation in the summer. The tours in this book are perfect "minivacations." Don't worry about the Saturday chores — do a midweek tidying of the house, pack on Thursday night, and hit the road at 5 P.M. on Friday (then hide your watch until late Sunday).

You'll discover that New England has enough diversity for even the most imaginative traveler. We confidently claim a variety unmatched by any other area of its size. A traveler can go from the mountains to the sea in a few short hours of driving. With us you'll spend a morning with Pilgrims at Plimoth Plantation and the afternoon browsing contemporary galleries in Provincetown. Or shop Burlington's lively pedestrian mall and in an hour find yourself in the unspoiled natural beauty of the Champlain islands. The 25 tours here are created to work comfortably in a weekend and guarantee the traveler a healthy dose of New England's treasures. We also offer a day trip for each state. These tours are hand picked to capture the essence of the state's character. (In Rhode Island we share what we think is the best ocean view in the Ocean State.)

We encourage you to customize our itineraries to your tastes. We have designed these tours to be a nice mix — some structure, some wandering, and lots of freedom. We've saved you time (and hassle) by recommending lodging and eating establishments but have given you enough options to make this trip your own. For a real New England experience, blend these weekend tours for an unbeatable vacation. Merge our Maine getaways, and at the end of this trip you'll know the state so well that you'll consider yourself an insider.

We promise you lighthouses, covered bridges, great views, country roads, and plenty of shopping, lodging, and eating suggestions. But remember that these tours are our favorites — so you'll find much, much more. We have gone to our trusted writers, editors, and friends for secrets that only folks who truly know an area can disclose. Jud Hale, longtime editor of *Yankee* and *The Old Farmer's Almanac,* tells us where to find the best Wiener schnitzel in New Hampshire. Marina Andrews makes your mouth water for the sweetest strawberries you'll ever taste, those that she and her family grow and sell in East Falmouth, Massachusetts. In the process of editing this book, we have talked to town clerks, librarians, curators, shopkeepers, and local residents. Wherever a tour takes you, know that we have gone ahead and asked locals for the special things — a picnic spot, crafts gallery, or corner sandwich shop — that make their towns unique. We often start our conversation by saying, "Where is the first place you'd take a dear friend who was visiting?" The answers are here, inside the pages of this book. We encourage you to ask the same. You'll find as we do that most local folks are generous (and just a little bit proud). Wherever you see the symbol "What the Locals Know," you're in for a surprise.

In addition, we offer updated addresses, phone numbers, hours, and prices for more than 600 inns, B&Bs, restaurants, stores, and historic and scenic attractions across New England. These are the "essentials" that follow every tour, and they include current access information as well as numbers for local travel resources. Restaurant prices: $ — most entrées under $10; $$ — most entrées $10-$16; $$$ — most entrées $17-$23; $$$$ — over $23. Just a bit of advice, though — things *do* change, so the wise traveler knows to call ahead, especially if traveling midweek or off-season.

Speaking of seasons, you'll notice as you browse the table of contents that some of the tours are season specific. What that means is that we know these tours are especially rewarding then, but we well know that our favorite foliage tour in Vermont is also a terrific trail to follow during maple sugaring. And then in summer, too, when clear and deep tree-lined ponds glisten, making the perfect backdrop for a picnic and a swim. The book that I wished I once had is now in your hands. Meander with us and forge your own new trails. We'll be looking for you.

– Polly Bannister

Maine

Portland, a Fall Weekend of Architecture and Great Food

PROFESSIONAL CYNIC AMBROSE BIERCE ONCE DEFINED November as the "eleventh twelfth of a weariness." Few New Englanders would dispute that. After October the countryside becomes mournful and barren, and the sky takes on a permanent pewter cast. Once-healthy complexions begin to resemble alabaster. What's a traveler to do?

Here's a suggestion: Spend a weekend in Portland, a trip you could never quite justify when beach and backyard beckoned. Portland is a lively year-round city that refuses to adopt that forlorn, abandoned look when the last tourist heads south after Columbus Day. In fact, it positively blossoms in the fall. The Portland Symphony and two theater companies launch new schedules. The pace at the restaurants becomes more comfortable and relaxed. Pubs and taverns that were virtually deserted in the sunny days of summer start filling with local faces like a months-long family reunion. And the thin November light seems to imbue the brick cityscape with a subtle, attenuated glow.

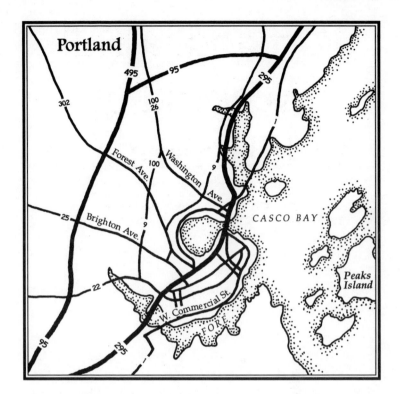

Day One

Plan to arrive in Portland Friday late afternoon or early evening. (Don't worry about rush hour. There isn't one.) As you pull into town, you'll see the towering white Holiday Inn, which looks a bit as if it were moved here by barge from Fort Lauderdale. It offers good views of the bay, but you'd be better served at the handful of smaller inns with more flair and charm. Your best bet: head to the **Pomegranate Inn** in Portland's elegant West End, a 15-minute walk from downtown (where parking is no problem now, either). Isabel Smiles has created a visually stunning interior invested with exuberant colors and bold forms. Housed in a fine old manse in a quiet neighborhood, the inn's overall effect borders on the magical. Some rooms have fireplaces, and all rooms are air-conditioned.

Other neighborhood inns include the **West End Inn,** a homey B&B in a Victorian town house, and the **Inn on Carleton,** built in 1869 and now owned and operated by Sue Cox. Those looking for a more urban experience might be tempted by the **Portland Regency Inn,** located in a converted armory in the heart of the Old Port. One note: If you opt for downtown, expect a fair amount of rowdiness outside your window late into the night.

Once you've settled in, you might start thinking about a boiled lobster dinner. Well, forget about it. You can buy a lobster before you leave and cook it at home. Portland's restaurant scene is too creative and spirited to bypass while you're here. Instead, walk the few blocks to either the **West Side** or **Katahdin.** Both feature New American cuisine: West Side specializes in fresh Maine game, and they do accept reservations; Katahdin's emphasis is on local produce, and they do not accept reservations.

Day Two

Put on a heavy sweater and start the day with a walking tour of Portland's Western Promenade. Ask Isabel at the Pomegranate Inn to lend you Greater Portland Landmark's descriptive brochure of the neighborhood; it is a virtual catalog of architectural styles. Homes range from imposing Georgian mansions heavy with classical elements to whimsical Gothic cottages. Be sure to wander down Bowdoin Street with its distinctive shingle-style homes, many of which were designed in the 1880s by local architect John Calvin Stevens. The architect himself lived at No. 52.

Next, head for an architectural monument of a decidedly different sort at the **Portland Museum of Art,** designed by I. M. Pei Associates. Once this modern, open building tended to outshine its art, but that changed with the addition of the Payson collection of Impressionist works and the recent bequest of 66 American works from philanthropist Elizabeth Noyce. You'll enjoy paintings by Jamie and N. C.

Portland Head Light was first illuminated in 1791, making it Maine's oldest lighthouse. A museum is housed in the former keeper's house. (courtesy Portland Convention & Visitors Bureau)

Wyeth, Childe Hassam, Fitz Hugh Lane, and selections from Maine artists Marsden Hartley, Winslow Homer, and Andrew Wyeth. If you're traveling with children, don't miss the **Children's Museum** next door. This exceptionally well-designed museum has as its chief attraction a top-floor camera obscura that creates a tabletop "movie" of real-life downtown Portland. But there's lots more to see — a space-shuttle cockpit, fire poles, a news center, computer learning activities, and Main Street exhibit with shops.

After you've had your fill of art, wander down Congress Street for a bite to eat. At 579 you'll find the **Starlight Café.** A few blocks away is the **Thos. Moser Store,** famous for its elegant and spare wooden furniture. The store

SOME OTHER GOOD PLACES TO EAT IN PORTLAND

WHAT THE LOCALS KNOW

Café Uffa!, 190 State St. Tucked away in one of Portland's more "rustic" neighborhoods, funky Café Uffa! knows how to work a fish over a wood grill better than any other place on the seacoast. It's also reasonably priced, offering one of the best dining deals in Maine. Open for dinner Wednesday-Saturday, for brunch Sunday. $-$$. 207-775-3380.

Fore Street, 288 Fore St. This huge loft-size industrial space a block off Portland's waterfront is anchored by a bustling open grill and kitchen smack in the middle. The evening twilight is magical, as is the food, and the seafood is especially well prepared. Open for dinner nightly. $$-$$$. 207-775-2717.

Silly's, 40 Washington Ave. Budget-minded diners in the know flock here for casual noshing at its most creative. Enjoy grilled lamb wrapped in pita bread and fresh milkshakes, as Tracy Chapman croons in the background. Think of it as a humble lunch stand with a college degree. Open Monday-Saturday 10-10. $-$$. 207-772-0360.

Three Dollar Dewey's, 241 Commercial St. Walk in and eye the long tables, the popcorn machine, the forest of beer taps behind the bar, and you'll think: Hmmm, looks like a great place for an ale. But don't stop there — the creative bar menu boasts the best french fries in Portland. Open for lunch and dinner daily. $-$$. 207-772-3310.

Amato's Italian Sandwich Shops, 1379 Washington Ave. and 71 India St. Local lore has it that the Italian sandwich was invented in Portland in 1899 by a baker named Giovanni Amato as a portable and inexpensive lunch for construction workers. Here you'll find the sandwich in all its glory and variations. Open Sunday-Thursday 6 A.M.-midnight, Friday-Saturday 6-1 A.M. 207-797-5514.

Port Bakehouse, 205 Commercial St. Cream-cheese brownies, gooey cookies, and other goodies. Also open for lunches. Bakery open Monday-Friday 7:30-5:30, Saturday 8-5, Sunday 8:30-3. 207-773-2217.

Becky's, 390 Commercial St. A waterfront diner where there's always a line for breakfast. Enormous portions; great prices. Opens daily at 4 A.M. 207-773-7070.

earned its reputation with Shaker-inspired chairs as refined as the originals but a far cry more comfortable. Moser recently branched out with a new line of furniture based on Arts and Crafts-style chairs and tables, all of which are neatly displayed in a meticulously renovated historic brick building.

The rest of the afternoon? It's your call. You might wander down to the brick-and-cobblestone Old Port to browse the shops, which include an array of boutiques and art galleries. You'll find everything from extraordinary contemporary crafts to kitschy knickknacks and most everything in between. (Be sure to note the intricate brickwork on the buildings, most of which were built after the devastating 1866 fire.) For gorgeous crafts, you won't find better shopping than **Abacus** and **Nancy Margolis Gallery.** The jewelry of Maine artists is the specialty at **Fibula,** and a little off the path near the West End is a fun gallery called **Delilah Pottery.** If your tastes tend toward the literary, plan to while away the hours before the early November dusk exploring Portland's half-dozen excellent used-book stores, which are growing in number and reputation. Among the best: **Carlson & Turner Books, Emerson Booksellers,** and **Harding's Book Shop.**

After resting up, pick a dining spot according to your budget. Among the better restaurants in town are **Back Bay Grill,** where chef Larry Matthews concentrates on New American cuisine with regional influences, and **Mozon Middle,** which challenges culinary limits by mixing classical regional dishes with elements borrowed from other cultures. Both are also expensive by Portland standards, but neither will disappoint. For those on a tighter budget, consider **Pepperclub,** which features world cuisine with a focus on vegetarian dishes.

If you've got any energy left after dinner, pick up a copy of *Casco Bay Weekly,* a widely distributed free newspaper, and peruse the entertainment calendar. And of course, there's always the movie option. Downtown Portland has seven screens, most of which show foreign or art films. For schedules, call **The Movies** or **Nickelodeon.**

Day Three

If the weather's agreeable, wander down to the **Casco Bay Lines** ferry terminal on Commercial Street and hop on the 20-minute ferry to Peaks Island. Spend some time exploring this turn-of the-century summer resort, now populated with a sizable contingent of year-round commuters. Quiet roads lead past eclectic Victorian cottages to overgrown World War II fortifications surrounded by marsh.

More goal-oriented walkers might prefer the four-mile loop road encircling the island. Take time to enjoy the views of even more remote islands and to explore the tide pools along the rocky back shore. Added bonus: the year-round residents have normally recovered from the shock of the summer influx by November and tend to be more relaxed and charitable to visitors than during the midsummer crush.

Before you leave for home, don't forget to pick up those lobsters to go. Several places along Commercial Street on Portland's waterfront will pack them for travel. Lobster prices usually hit rock bottom in the fall, offering a low-cost way to appear magnanimous to friends and neighbors back home. Splurge on a dozen.

– Wayne Curtis

E s s e n t i a l s

Convention and Visitors Bureau of Greater Portland, 305 Commercial St., Portland, ME 04101. 207-772-5800.

Greater Portland Landmarks, 165 State St., Portland, ME 04101. 207-774-5561.

Portland's Downtown District, 400 Congress St., Portland, ME 04101. 207-772-6828.

Pomegranate Inn, 49 Neal St. Double room with breakfast $95-$135. 800-356-0408, 207-772-1006.

West End Inn, 146 Pine St. Double room with breakfast $119-$129. 800-338-1377, 207-772-1377.

Inn on Carleton, 46 Carleton St. Double room with breakfast $119-$129. 800-639-1779, 207-775-1910.

Portland Regency Inn, 20 Milk St. Double room $139-$159. 800-727-3436, 207-774-4200.

West Side, 58 High St. Open for dinner Tuesday-Sunday. $$-$$$. 207-773-8223.

Katahdin, 106 High St. Open for dinner Tuesday-Thursday 5-9:30, Friday-Saturday 5-10:30. $$. 207-774-1740.

Portland Museum of Art, 7 Congress Sq. Open Tuesday, Wednesday, Saturday 10-5; Thursday and Friday 10-9. Adults $6, seniors $5, children 6-12 $1, under 6 free. 207-773-2787.

Children's Museum of Maine, 142 Free St. Open daily 10-5, Sunday noon-5. Adults $5, under 1 free. 207-828-1234.

Starlight Café, 579 Congress St. Open Monday-Friday 7-3. $. 207-775-7827.

Thos. Moser Store, 415 Cumberland Ave. Open Monday-Saturday 9-5. 207-774-3791.

Abacus, 44 Exchange St. Open Monday-Wednesday 10-6; Thursday, Friday, Saturday 10-9; Sunday 11-6. 207-772-4880.

Nancy Margolis Gallery, 367 Fore St. Open Monday-Wednesday 10-6, Thursday-Saturday 10-8, Sunday noon-5. 207-775-3822.

Fibula, 50 Exchange St. Open Monday-Saturday 10-6. 207-761-4432.

Delilah Pottery, 134 Spring St. Open Tuesday-Friday 11-6, Saturday noon-4. 207-871-1594.

Carlson & Turner Books, 241 Congress St. Open Monday-Saturday 10-5, Sunday noon-5. 800-540-7323, 207-773-4200.

Emerson Booksellers, 420 Fore St. Open Monday-Saturday 11-5, Sunday noon-5. 207-874-2665.

Harding's Book Shop, 538 Congress St. Open Monday-Saturday 10-5:30. 207-761-2150.

Back Bay Grill, 65 Portland St. Open for dinner Monday-Thursday 5:30-9:30, Friday-Saturday 5:30-10. $$$. 207-772-8833.

Mozon Middle, 47 Middle St. Open for dinner Tuesday-Saturday 5-9. $$-$$$. 207-774-9399.

Pepperclub, 78 Middle St. Open for dinner daily. $-$$. 207-772-0531.

The Movies, 10 Exchange St. 207-772-9600.

Nickelodeon, corner Temple and Middle sts. 207-772-9751.

Casco Bay Lines, 56 Commercial St. Open daily; $3 round-trip to Peaks Island; call for ferry service schedule. 207-774-7871.

Peninsular Wanderings in Casco Bay

MAINE'S COASTAL GEOGRAPHY CONFOUNDS SIMPLE, tidy trips. The long, narrow peninsulas with relatively few bridges spanning coastal rivers can make for frustrating rambling — but also create cultural cul-de-sacs, where strip malls and the less endearing aspects of modern-day life haven't yet caught up with the past.

Maine has one such area just a half hour north of Portland: the Harpswell peninsula. Harpswell is actually three distinct peninsulas that thrust downward into Casco Bay like the prongs of a pitchfork. (One peninsula is in fact two islands, Orrs and Bailey, linked by bridges.) While convoluted — exploring involves dead ends and backtracking — the area is blessedly compact. Visitors can find a suitable base lodge and spend one day exploring the coastal area and one day exploring the inland towns. Or reverse the route if the weather doesn't cooperate.

Day One

Plan to arrive in mid-coast Maine by late afternoon. If you're so inclined, exit I-95 at Freeport for a stop at **L.L. Bean** and the hundred or so other outlets in the area that range from

Calvin Klein and Ralph Lauren to Reebok and Patagonia. Even with its far-flung reputation as a shopping mecca, Freeport has by and large managed to retain the dignity and grace of a small town, although recent mall-like encroachments south of town make some folks nervous. To make things easy on yourself, find the Hose Tower Information Center on the west side of Main Street for a good map, nearby parking, rest rooms, a public phone, and an ATM. Don't forget to visit the **L.L. Bean Factory Store** (across Main Street from the retail store), where you'll find seconds and samples — no guarantees, but worth a look.

If you are traveling with kids, consider a stop at the **Desert of Maine,** where they can run off some steam at this 40-acre sand dune (a glacial plain). Kids love the gem hunt here and sand-art demonstrations. For an early dinner, the **Harraseeket Inn,** just around the corner from L.L. Bean, offers American fare (try the roast chicken for two) and superb desserts.

Follow Route 1 north to Brunswick, then backtrack south on Route 123 near Bowdoin College. The peninsulas reach down about 15 miles from here, with several inns and B&Bs along the way. The **Harpswell Inn** is situated on a peaceful country road in a 1761 house on the site of a former boatyard. The interior has been rather suburbanized and feels more like Westchester County than Colonial New England, but it's comfortable and eclectic and offers glimpses of Middle Bay. There's also a quiet trail along the water. Two guest suites in a made-over carriage house are worth a splurge.

For more remote lodging, try the creaky **Driftwood Inn,** a compound of weathered shingled buildings set on three acres at the end of a winding road on Bailey Island. The accommodations are classic summer cottage: exposed pine beams, wicker chairs, a small pool, and remarkable views of the rocky coast. Many of the spartan but generally comfortable rooms share bathrooms and showers, but some have their own toilets and sinks. Meals (not included in daily rate)

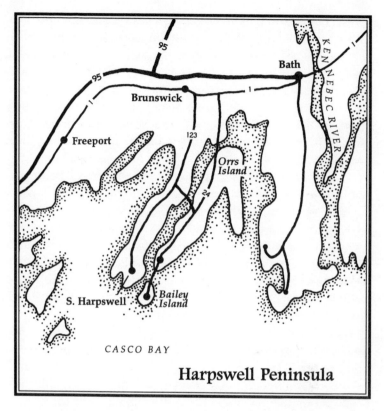

Harpswell Peninsula

are served in an austere dining room of time-burnished pine.

Bailey Island Motel offers more modern, predictable accommodations. On Route 24 near the bridge to Bailey Island, the motel is set off the road and on the water's edge, and it offers easy access to local attractions.

Day Two

Bikes are a good way to appreciate the subtle views. Pedal along the southern reaches, since the northerly sections of the roads are busier than many bikers will find comfortable. Whether by car or by bike, the terrain hereabouts is gentle and inviting. Don't expect the high cliffs and severe spires of spruce found farther Down East. Harpswell is meadows and forests of oak and maple. White clapboard houses proliferate away from the water, with simple shingled cottages closer to the sea. It's not hard to convince yourself that you're traveling some miles inland — until a view of a cobalt inlet lined with fractured, jet-black rock suddenly rises into view. Be sure to check out the unique Cribstone Bridge linking Bailey and Orrs islands. Built in 1928, the honeycomb of granite blocks allows the strong tides through without carrying the bridge away.

Plan for lunch at **Dolphin Marina** at Basin Point in South Harpswell. From the name you might envision fancy yachtsmen, but you'd be mistaken. This restaurant — overlooking meadows littered with boats coming out of the water for the season — has a simple interior of pine and Naugahyde. The marina is two miles off Route 123; heading south, turn right at the West Harpswell School onto Ash Point Road, then take another right on Basin Point Road. The old counter seats six, but hold out for one of the booths. Choose from sandwiches and fish stews, all of which are inexpensive and many of which are served with fresh blueberry muffins.

You won't get a sense of the slow pace of the peninsulas if you're rushing around by car. Be sure to pull off, park, and explore by foot at some point. A good spot for an afternoon stroll is among the scattered summer homes at the tip of South Harpswell.

For dinner: lobster, of course. On the Bailey Island side, head to **Cook's Lobster House,** located on the water with a view of the Cribstone Bridge. This huge establishment (it seats 280) specializes in seafood entrées served professionally and expeditiously and offers a variety of shore dinners involving lobster.

On the Harpswell side, the **Estes Lobster House** is another cavernous place, where you can eat a triple lobster plate with french fries and butter amid loud and jovial surroundings. Don't miss the model of the seven-masted *Thomas W. Larson* in the entryway.

Kids and adults alike enjoy strolling the 40 acres of mineral-rich glacial sand deposits at the Desert of Maine. (courtesy Desert of Maine)

Day Three

This is the day for exploring the two big towns. Start with a drive to Bath, and enjoy brunch at **Kristina's,** a restaurant in two connected houses. There's dining outside on a deck as well as in rambling rooms inside. Whatever your entrée, be sure to sample the famous pecan buns.

Walk through town and enjoy the simple brick architecture and the park along the Kennebec River; then visit the **Maine Maritime Museum,** just south of town on the river. This modern, sprawling museum fuels fantasies of setting sail for points unknown. The collections range from detailed oil paintings of famous sailing ships to more practical displays of shipbuilding in the outbuildings on the grounds (the site of a former busy shipyard).

When you've had your fill of seafaring, head back toward Brunswick for a trip to the Arctic. On the leafy campus of Bowdoin College is the small but intriguing **Peary-MacMillan Arctic Museum,** named after alumni Robert

Peary (class of 1877) and Donald MacMillan (class of 1898), who blazed trails in Arctic exploration in the late 19th and early 20th centuries. Learn about both men and how they survived in the inhospitable northern latitudes.

The **Bowdoin College Museum of Art,** in the Walker Art Building, is as notable for its graceful architecture (designed by the firm of McKim, Mead, and White) as for its collections. Among the artists represented are Winslow Homer and John Singleton Copley.

To cure your museum legs, walk down the gentle hill from the college to Brunswick's central shopping area, which flanks the wide expanse of Maine Street. There are several galleries, including the **Wyler Gallery,** with contemporary crafts by local artists. Stop by **Gulf of Maine** for a selection of volumes — many focusing on the environment — that you won't find at a mall bookshop.

Before heading home, try the funky **Miss Brunswick Diner** on Route 1 south of town for classic diner fare.

– Wayne Curtis

E s s e n t i a l s

Chamber of Commerce of the Bath-Brunswick Region, 59 Pleasant St., Brunswick, ME 04011. 207-725-8797.

Chamber of Commerce of the Bath-Brunswick Region, 45 Front St., Bath, ME 04530. 207-443-9751.

L.L. Bean, 95 Main St., Freeport. Open every day 24 hours. 800-341-4341.

L.L. Bean Factory Store, Depot St., Freeport. Open daily 10-10. 800-341-4341.

Desert of Maine, Desert Rd., Freeport (2.5 miles from downtown). Open daily mid-May to mid-October 9 A.M.- sunset. Adults $4.75, seniors $4.25, children $2.75. 207-865-6962.

Harraseeket Inn, 162 Main St., Freeport. Open for dinner nightly 6-9. $$$. 207-865-9377.

Harpswell Inn, 141 Lookout Point Rd., Harpswell. Double room $59-$116, suites $150, with breakfast. 800-843-5509, 207-833-5509.

Driftwood Inn, Washington Ave., Bailey Island. Double room $70-$75. $$. 207-833-5461.

Bailey Island Motel, Rte. 24, Bailey Island. Double room May-June 15 and October $70, June 15-September 30 $90. 207-833-2886.

Dolphin Marina, Basin Point, South Harpswell. Open daily 8-8. $-$$. 207-833-6000.

Cook's Lobster House, Garrison Cove Rd., Bailey Island. Open daily 11:30-8, Friday- Saturday 11:30-9. $$-$$$$. 207-833-6641.

Estes Lobster House, Rte. 123, South Harpswell. Open seasonally. $-$$$$. 207-833-6340.

Kristina's, 160 Centre St., Bath. Open every day 8 A.M.-8:30 P.M.; brunch weekends 9-2. $. 207-442-8577.

Maine Maritime Museum, 243 Washington St., Bath. Open daily 9:30-5. Adults $7.75, children 6-17 $5, under 6 free. 207-443-1316.

Peary-MacMillan Arctic Museum, Hubbard Hall, Bowdoin College, Brunswick. Open Tuesday-Saturday 10-5, Sunday 2-5. Free. 207-725-3416.

Bowdoin College Museum of Art, Walker Art Building, Bowdoin College, Brunswick. Open Tuesday-Saturday 10-5, Sunday 2-5. Free. 207-725-3275.

Wyler Gallery, 150 Maine St., Brunswick. Open Monday-Thursday 10-6, Friday 10-8, Saturday 10-5, Sunday 10-3. 207-729-1321.

Gulf of Maine, 134 Maine St., Brunswick. Open Monday-Saturday 9:30-5:30. 207-729-5083.

Miss Brunswick Diner, 101½ Pleasant St., Brunswick. Open Sunday-Thursday 5 A.M.-9 P.M., Friday-Saturday open 24 hours. 207-729-5948.

Timeless Towns Along the Coast from Port Clyde to Islesboro

THE LITTLE TOWNS THAT CLING TO THE STONY WESTERN shores and islands of Penobscot Bay are deceptively gracious. Like the airy windjammers that now drift over the bay on a summer day, the coastal towns were built for rougher work: fishing, boatbuilding, stone quarrying. And despite inroads of the 20th century, these small communities retain their simple, stunning architecture and their timeless connection to the sea.

Day One

If you can defer breakfast until you reach the tiny fishing village of Port Clyde, reward yourself with a platter of blueberry pancakes at the venerable **Ocean House Hotel,** where locals and guests alike start their day. Another breakfast option is to pour your own coffee and pull up a stool-with-a-view at the **Port Clyde General Store.** Port Clyde is a jumping-off point for Monhegan Island on the *Laura B.* or *Elizabeth Ann,* so expect waves of boat catchers. (The Ocean

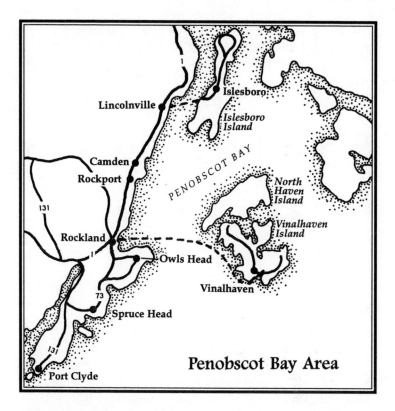

Penobscot Bay Area

House is a great place to stay if you are planning to take the morning ferry to Monhegan.)

Leaving Port Clyde, turn east on Route 73 for a pretty drive through Spruce Head and Owls Head. Adjacent to the Knox County Airport you'll find one of the country's best collections of antique cars and planes — in working order — at the **Owls Head Transportation Museum.** Here there's everything from horse-drawn carriages to bikes, motorcycles, and World War I fighter planes.

If you encounter rain or light fog as you approach the old shipbuilding town of Rockland, seize the excuse to savor the **Farnsworth Art Museum.** You'll find a stellar collection of works about Maine and by Maine artists, including three generations of Wyeths. Leave time to tour the neighboring

Farnsworth Homestead, an 1850 Greek Revival mansion reputed to house Rockland's first indoor plumbing.

Retreat for lunch and a slab of murderous Velvet Underground chocolate cake at **Second Read Books and Coffee.** Then visit the **Shore Village Museum,** Maine's lighthouse museum, to see fascinating, and surprisingly large, pieces of lighthouse innards and other historical oddities.

In the afternoon, park at the **Maine State Ferry Service,** at the north end of town, and set sail for an overnight in Vinalhaven, watching for seals in the ferry wake. (Taking a car is possible but not necessary.)

For lodging in Vinalhaven, the **Payne Homestead at Moses Webster House** is a Gothic wonder with stunning rooms (including a playroom) and a stretch of gorgeous garden at the door.

Vinalhaven's waters are home to an astonishing number of lobster boats, but its now-quiet quarries once yielded granite to build monuments all over the eastern seaboard. Don't miss the **Vinalhaven Historical Society Museum** on High Street.

During a fashion show at the Owls Head Transportation Museum women dress in period clothes, using a 1926 Pierce Arrow as a **backdrop.** *(courtesy Owls Head Transportation Museum)*

Despite its setting — a little like a cavernous room in a rustic summer cottage — the **Haven** is famous even on the mainland for its excellent and creative cuisine. For dinner, reserve a booth with a water view. Then put the edge on your appetite with an early-evening stroll out to Lane's Island Preserve. A 15-minute walk south on Atlantic Avenue will deliver you into an Andrew Wyeth painting, complete with long fields, a stony beach, and an old farmhouse on the hill.

Day Two

Catch a morning ferry back to the mainland, then drive up Route 1 to Rockport. Stop first at the Marine Park (turn right just before you cross the bridge into town) to pay respects to the statue of Andre the Seal and to see the stone kilns left from a booming lime industry. **Maine Coast Artists Gallery** features some of the state's best contemporary artists, and just up Central Street the Maine Photographic Workshops (a nationally known year-round school) has a gallery open to the public in the summer.

For lunch, stroll down to the **Sail Loft** for a cup of lobster stew with a view of Rockport Harbor. Or go on to Camden for other lunch choices, including down-home **Marriner's,** which boasts, "No ferns, no quiche," and keeps the locals slipping into its booths for simple seafood and sandwiches and great breakfasts. Camden's most popular lunch spot is **Cappy's Chowder House,** where you'll find croissant sandwiches, seafood stew made with local kielbasa, and chowder once noted in *Gourmet* magazine.

Like Rockport and Rockland, Camden launched its share of schooners, and tall ships still congregate here, as you'll discover when you explore the harbor. Then, as Camden's crowds build, wander the trails at **Merryspring Horticultural Nature Park,** a preserve dedicated to native flowers, herbs, and trees. Or drive north on Route 1 to **Camden Hills State Park** for a one-hour hike (you may also drive) up Mount Battie and a breathtaking view of the harbor and Penobscot Bay.

Lodging in Camden numbers in the dozens and ranges from motels to inns. The handsome and historic **Whitehall Inn** is seemingly unchanged since Edna St. Vincent Millay read her poem about the Camden Hills here in 1912. At the other end of the spectrum are the two motel-like rooms with waterfront balconies at the **Owl and Turtle Harbor View Guest Rooms** — the best views in town.

For dinner, head to **Frogwater Café** for very inventive fare at very reasonable prices. Seafood on the breezy terrace of the **Waterfront** is more elegant.

Day Three

It's a short drive to **Lincolnville Beach** for the ferry to Islesboro. The ferry docks near the wonderful **Grindle Point Sailor's Memorial Museum and Lighthouse.** Pick up a map of the island here. Refurbished exhibits at the **Islesboro Historical Society** trace the island's humble origins in farming, fishing, and shipbuilding. Drive north toward Pripet, the year-round end of the island, to find the society at the first stop sign. Continue through the Narrows and drive counterclockwise around the island; there's a historic cemetery as you head south and another on Meeting House Road near the end of the loop.

After passing back through the Narrows, stop at Dark Harbor Village. You can pick up a sandwich and ice cream at the **Dark Harbor Shop** or assemble a gourmet picnic at Four Shades of Purple (no phone). There's a lovely little beach at the island's south end. Drive there at a leisurely pace, taking time to ogle the stately old summer mansions of Dark Harbor on the way. But don't linger too long watching windjammers ply the sparkling water — the last boat leaves at 4:30!

– Hannah Holmes

MORE WYETHS IN MAINE

The Farnsworth Museum opens its new Center for the Wyeth Family in the summer of 1998. The center, located in a new building adjoined to the existing museum, will display collections of artwork by and research materials on three generations of America's most prominent artistic dynasty: N. C. Wyeth (1882-1945), Andrew (born 1917), and Jamie (born 1946). The Wyeth family has contributed significantly to the center by providing several thousand paintings, drawings, prints, and archive materials. The Wyeths have had a long-standing connection to the museum since 1944, when the Farnsworth purchased three watercolors by Andrew for its collection. The Farnsworth also owns and operates the Olson House in nearby Cushing, the site of Andrew Wyeth's best-known painting, *Christina's World* (1948), now in the Museum of Modern Art.

Farnsworth Center for the Wyeth Family in Maine, 352 Main St., Rockland. 207-596-6457.

N. C. Wyeth painted **Bright and Fair — Eight Bells** *in 1936. It was his family home and studio in Port Clyde, Maine.* (courtesy Farnsworth Art Museum)

Essentials

Rockland-Thomaston Chamber of Commerce, P.O. Box 508, Rockland, ME 04841. 207-596-0376.

Rockport-Camden-Lincolnville Chamber of Commerce, P.O. Box 919, Camden, ME 04843. 207-236-4404.

Maine Windjammers Association. No arguing that a wind-jammer cruise is the best way to see the Maine coast. 800-807-9463, 207-374-5400.

Ocean House Hotel, Rte. 131, Port Clyde. Open May 1-Columbus Day. 800-269-6691, 207-372-6691.

Port Clyde General Store, 1 City Ctr. Open daily 7 A.M.-8 P.M. 207-372-6543.

Monhegan Boat Lines, end of Rte. 131, Port Clyde. Three ferries daily: 7 A.M., 10:30 A.M., and 2:30 P.M. Adults $25 round-trip, children 12 and under $12. 207-372-8848.

Owls Head Transportation Museum, Rte. 73, Owls Head. Open daily year-round, April-October 10-5, November-March 10-3. Adults $5, children $3, under 5 free. 207-594-4418.

Farnsworth Art Museum, 352 Main St., Rockland. Open Monday-Saturday 9-5, Sunday noon-5. Adults $5, seniors $4, children 8-18 $3, under 8 free. 207-596-6457.

Second Read Books and Coffee, 328 Main St., Rockland. Open daily 11-4:30. 207-594-4123.

Shore Village Museum, 104 Limerock St., Rockland. Open June-October 10-4. Donation. 207-594-0311.

Maine State Ferry Service, 517A Main St., Rockland. Adults $9, children $4, autos $26, parking $4. 207-596-2202.

Payne Homestead at Moses Webster House, Atlantic Ave., Vinalhaven. Double room with breakfast $75-$95. 888-863-9963, 207-863-9963.

Vinalhaven Historical Society Museum, High St., Vinalhaven. Open daily 11-3 or by appointment. 207-863-4410.

Haven, 245 Main St., Vinalhaven. Open daily for dinner. $$-$$$. 207-863-4969.

Maine Coast Artists Gallery, 162 Russell Ave., Rockport. Open Tuesday-Saturday 10-5. Donation $2. 207-236-2875.

Sail Loft, 1 Main St., Rockport. Open for lunch daily 11:30-2:30, dinner daily 5:30-8:30. $$-$$$. 207-236-2330.

Marriner's, 35 Main St., Camden. Open daily 6-2. 207-236-2647.

Cappy's Chowder House, Main St., Camden. Open daily year-round, Monday-Saturday 11-10, Sunday 9 A.M.-10 P.M., Sunday brunch 9-noon. 207-236-2254.

Merryspring Horticultural Nature Park, end of Conway Rd. off Rte. 1S, Camden. 207-236-2239.

Camden Hills State Park, Rte. 1, Camden. Adults $2, seniors free, children 50¢, prices subject to change. 207-236-3109.

Whitehall Inn, 52 High St., Camden. Double room with breakfast $65-$145. 800-789-6565, 207-236-3391.

Owl and Turtle Harbor View Guest Rooms, 8 Bayview, Camden. Double room with continental breakfast $85-$95. 207-236-9014, 207-236-8759.

Frogwater Café, 31 Elm St., Camden. Open for lunch and dinner Tuesday-Sunday. $-$$. 207-236-8998.

Waterfront, 62 Bayview, Camden. Open for dinner daily 5-10. $$. 207-236-3747.

Lincolnville Beach — Ferry to Islesboro. Adults $4.50, children $2, car $13, car reservation $5 (reserve car well in advance). 207-789-5611, 207-734-6935.

Grindle Point Sailor's Memorial Museum and Lighthouse, Islesboro. Open Tuesday-Sunday 9-4:30. Free.

Islesboro Historical Society. Open Sunday-Thursday 12:30-4:30. Donation. 207-734-6733.

Dark Harbor Shop, Islesboro. 207-734-8878.

Stunning Vistas and Fine Food in the Rangeley Lakes Region

A DRIVE THROUGH THE WESTERN MOUNTAINS OF MAINE in the fall has all the things a visitor would want: foliage, vistas, good inns and restaurants, interesting side trips, pretty towns small enough to stroll through in an hour. And lacks the things you don't want: crowds and stoplights. It is such a pleasant drive that it comes with the highest recommendation of all — even a local might be inspired to take it on a sunny fall weekend.

Day One

Start from exit 12 on the Maine Turnpike in Auburn. Follow the signs for Route 4 to the north, and after you pass beyond the city limits of Auburn, you'll be free. Travel along this route as it narrows and twists, stopping to visit the permanent yard sales and secondhand shops that dot the landscape like native vegetation. Continue north on Route 4 to where it joins Route 2 and travel east to Farmington. After crossing the Sandy River bridge, turn left on Route 27/4, and

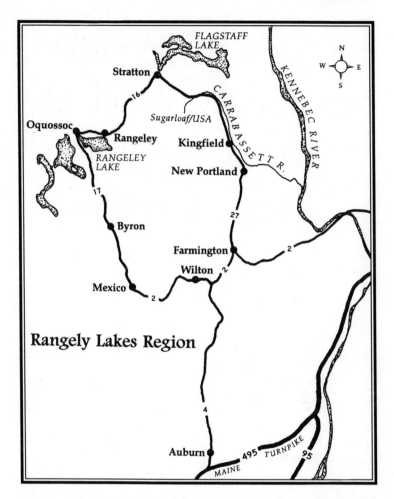

FLAGSTAFF LAKE

Stratton

16

Sugarloaf/USA

Oquossoc

Rangeley

Kingfield

RANGELEY LAKE

New Portland

CARRABASSETT R.

KENNEBEC RIVER

17

Byron

27

Farmington

2

Wilton

2

Mexico

2

Rangely Lakes Region

4

Auburn

495

TURNPIKE

95

MAINE

at the only stoplight in town, turn right for lunch at the **Homestead Bakery Restaurant,** which serves some exotic fare for this part of Maine.

After lunch, continue north on Route 27/4 and turn right on Holley Road to visit the **Nordica Homestead Museum.** The 1857 birthplace of Lillian Nordica, the first internationally known American opera star, exhibits memorabilia from her career.

Return to Route 27/4 and shortly turn right onto Route

27, north toward Kingfield. This is where your drive begins to be ever more relaxing and beautiful. The western mountains will draw closer and closer, and the open spaces become more frequent and larger. Keep an eye out for moose, especially along the low-lying stretches of road. In New Portland turn right and follow signs for the Wire Bridge, one of the few wire suspension bridges left in the country (it looks like a very miniature Golden Gate Bridge). The attraction here is more than its construction — walk out onto the bridge and you'll have a fantastic view up and down the Carrabassett River. It is also a favorite picnic and swimming spot among locals.

Back on Route 27 now, and the day is wearing on, so plan to overnight in Kingfield, an oasis of fine dining and lovely inns in the open spaces of this part of Maine. One of the finest meals in the state can be had at **One Stanley Avenue,** just across the bridge on Route 16. Chef/owner Dan Davis has created a singular menu, featuring dishes with Maine flavors (fiddleheads, maple chicken) in a restored Victorian that combines formal dining with a relaxed atmosphere. After dinner you can stay next door at **Three Stanley Avenue,** the unpretentious B&B also owned by Davis.

Other dining and overnighting options in the area include the **Inn on Winter's Hill, Longfellow's,** and the **Herbert Hotel,** all within walking distance (everything in Kingfield is within walking distance).

If you are interested in lodging "on mountain" rather than in town, **Sugarloaf/USA** offers hundreds of rooms in their inn and condominiums. Here you'll find all the luxuries — a sports and fitness center, hot tubs, sauna, steam room, and pool. If you play golf, it doesn't get any better than the 18 holes at the **Sugarloaf Golf Club.** This course was designed by Robert Trent Jones II, whose unique flair with bunkers and undulations has earned him the reputation of being one of the country's most creative designers. Each hole here is nearly unto itself and framed by white birch trees that give players a feeling of absolute privacy. The

Sugarloaf pro reports that golfers are always enthusiastic about the 10th (par 4) and 11th (par 3) holes, where there is a 125-foot drop in elevation from tee to green. The six holes on the back nine, which run adjacent to the Carrabassett River, are known as "a string of pearls."

Day Two

Begin the day with a visit to the **Stanley Museum,** dedicated to the accomplishments of the Stanleys, natives of Kingfield. The family included the Stanley twins, Francis and Freelan, builders of the Stanley Steamer automobile, and their sister, Chansonetta Stanley Emmons, a pioneer photographer.

When you are finished browsing, head northwest toward Canada, to which you are getting temptingly close. But stay on this side of the border, following the lovely Carrabassett River to Stratton, on the shores of Flagstaff Lake. Right now might be a good time to eat, and there are a couple of modest places to choose from, both on Main Street: the **Stratton Plaza Hotel** and **White Wolf Inn and Café.**

After lunch, visit the Dead River Historical Society (at the junction of routes 27 and 16) if it's open. Then turn left

---

 A SOPHISTICATED SURPRISE

Just outside of Kingfield you'll find Ritzo Royall Studio Gallery, where partners Patty Ritzo, a pastel painter, and Jan Royall, stained-glass artist, offer their creations plus hundreds of finely crafted works by local artists. This is an exceptional collection of high-quality crafts from pottery to rustic furniture, to fine woodworking, to sculpture, weaving, turned bowls, and many other wonderful items. Locals say the gallery, which is located in a brick mansion built by a lumber baron in the 1830s for his daughters, is the closest thing to an art museum the town has.

Ritzo Royall Studio Gallery, North Main St. (Rte. 27 north). Open Thursday-Tuesday 11-5:30. 207-265-5626.

(west) on Route 16 to drive along the south branch of the Dead River. It is only 19 miles from here to the town of Rangeley, but take your time. You're in no hurry, and it's a pretty drive, especially in fall.

When you arrive in Rangeley, you may feel as though you took a wrong turn somewhere and ended up on an island: You are now in the heart of the Rangeley Lakes region. At this time of year lodging shouldn't be a problem. Check out the **Rangeley Inn** first; it is old and dignified, there are a zillion rooms, and it is not too pricey. If not there, try the **Rangeley Manor** or the **Country Club Inn.** There are several B&Bs in the area as well.

A full range of dining possibilities begins with the Rangeley Inn's sophisticated dining room and continues to the **Red Onion Restaurant.**

If you have time, drive a few miles up Route 4 to the home and workshop of Wilhelm Reich, the controversial scientist/psychologist. Called **Orgonon,** the 200-acre property has nature trails, a bookstore, and a splendid view. For an even greater view of the seven lakes, numerous ponds, and fir-covered mountains, take a scenic flight with **Mountain Air Service.** You might also enjoy just walking around the town of Rangeley (check out the fieldstone walls of the public library on Lake Street).

Day Three

The next morning, when you leave town, drive west on Route 16/4 to Oquossoc, which you may not notice if you blink. If you are ambitious and feel up to a short hike, continue straight on 4 past the routes 4 and 17 intersection, toward Haines Landing. It is only about a mile or so until you come to Bald Mountain Road. Turn left, drive a mile and a half, and look for the Bald Mountain Trailhead on your left. Park your car along the road and take the one-mile hike (1,000-foot elevation gain), which is moderately steep in some places.

After your hike, return to Route 17 and head south. Within the next ten miles there are two points, one on each side of the road, from which spectacular views can be had. My personal favorite is on the right (west), from which you can see all of the Rangeley Lakes, except Rangeley Lake itself. If you happen to be here at sunset, you are in for a real treat.

Farther down Route 17 you'll come to Byron, a teensy village. Stop at the roadside rest on the left next to Coos Canyon, a hard rock channel where the Swift River passes, creating several impressive falls. (This area is said to be the first spot in America where gold was discovered.) In Mexico turn left at the light onto Route 2, and follow it back to Wilton, where you can return to the Maine Turnpike on Route 4.

– Michael Burke

Essentials

Sugarloaf Area Chamber of Commerce, RR 1, Box 2151, Carrabassett Valley, ME 04947. 207-235-2100.

Rangeley Lakes Region Chamber of Commerce, P.O. Box 317, Rangeley, ME 04970. 800-MT-LAKES, 207-864-5364.

Homestead Bakery Restaurant, 20 Broadway, Farmington. Open daily for lunch 11-2, dinner 5-9. $-$$. 207-778-6162.

Nordica Homestead Museum, Holley Rd., Farmington. Open June 1-Labor Day Tuesday-Saturday 10-noon, Sunday 1-5. Adults $2, children $1. 207-778-2042.

One Stanley Avenue, 1 Stanley Ave., Kingfield. Open for dinner. $$$-$$$$. 207-265-5541.

Three Stanley Avenue, 3 Stanley Ave., Kingfield. Double room with breakfast $50-$60. 207-265-5541.

Inn on Winter's Hill, Winter's Hill, Kingfield. Double room $75-$125. 207-265-5421.

Longfellow's, Rte. 27, Kingfield. Open daily 11-9. $-$$. 207-265-4394.

Herbert Hotel, Main St., Kingfield. Double room with continental breakfast $49-$99. Open for dinner Thursday-Sunday 5:30-9. $$-$$$. 207-265-2000.

Sugarloaf/USA Inn and Condominiums, Carrabassett Valley. Double room $90-$185 (lower rates in summer). 800-THE-LOAF, 207-237-2000.

Sugarloaf Golf Club, Sugarloaf/USA. 207-237-2000.

Stanley Museum, School St., Kingfield. Open May-October Tuesday-Sunday 1-4. Donations. 207-265-2729.

Stratton Plaza Hotel, Main St., Stratton. Open daily, serving all day. $-$$. 207-246-2000.

White Wolf Inn and Café, Main St., Stratton. Open daily, lunch and dinner weekdays; breakfast, lunch, and dinner Saturday and Sunday. $-$$. 207-246-2922.

Rangeley Inn, Main St., Rangeley. Double room $69-$119. $$-$$$. 207-864-3341.

Rangeley Manor, off Main St., Rangeley. Cabins $70-$80. 207-864-3340.

Country Club Inn, Country Club Dr., Rangeley. Room with full breakfast $99 per person. 207-864-3831.

Red Onion Restaurant, Main St., Rangeley. Open daily 11-9. $-$$. 207-864-5022.

Orgonon, Dodge Pond Rd., off Rte. 4/16, Rangeley. Open July-August Tuesday-Sunday 1-5, September open only Sunday 1-5. Adults $3. 207-864-3443.

Mountain Air Service, 96 Main St., Rangeley. Operates daily, all year, $40 per person, $25 each for two or three people. 207-864-5307.

Making Magic on Mount Desert

THE CONVENTIONAL PLAN FOR VISITING MOUNT DESERT
Island (staying in Bar Harbor and driving the Park Loop
Road in Acadia National Park) certainly has its merits —
there wouldn't be so much traffic if it didn't. But there are
other ways to sample the craggy charms of Mount Desert.
This itinerary uses Somes Sound — the long fjord that nearly
bisects the island — as a buffer. You stay on the calmer side
of the island, venturing into mainstream attractions through
the back door.

Day One

Route 3 passes over tiny Thompson Island between the
mainland and Mount Desert; stop here at the **National
Park Information Center** to pick up a map of Acadia and a
copy of the *Acadia Beaver Log*, a monthly guide to activities
led by National Park Service rangers. When you cross the
bridge to Mount Desert, bear right onto Route 102 and
make a beeline down the west side of Somes Sound, which
divides the tranquil western side from the bustle of Bar
Harbor and Acadia on the east. In just eight miles you'll
reach Southwest Harbor.

This fishing, boatbuilding, and yachting village is the
(relatively) poor cousin of tony Northeast Harbor on the
other side of the sound. Southwest Harbor balances Mount
Desert's two industries: tourism and fishing. It's far enough

from the crowds so you can find parking and close enough to offer dining and shopping amenities that smaller villages lack.

You have a choice between two excellent B&Bs just south of the village. The elegant **Victorian Inn at Southwest,** where Jill Lewis is innkeeper, boasts beautiful parlors and nine bright and spacious rooms, each with private bath. Across the street, the rambling **Penury Hall Bed & Breakfast** has three rooms sharing two baths and a pair of cats. Hosts Gretchen and Toby Strong treat guests as honorary family members, "except they don't have to do the dishes."

Spend a bit of the afternoon walking from the sail-strewn harbor (with docks that service both work-worn fishing vessels and gleaming yachts) to the vintage small-town Main Street. The **Wendell Gilley Museum of Bird Carving** displays the highest achievements of this specialized craft.

You may be itching for a saltwater experience, but the swimming is far more comfortable in warmer fresh water at **Echo Lake,** sandwiched between high hills. If you've chosen Penury Hall, ask if the canoe is available, since Echo Lake also has splendid paddling along its shores. The lake and surrounding hillsides constitute one of the pieces of Acadia National Park that float free from the concentrated portion of the park on the east side of the island.

If it's Friday and you must have a great sunset picture, call 207-288-5262 to see if the Kodak film people are conducting a sunset photography workshop at the summit of Cadillac Mountain at 7:15. But before heading out, make a late reservation for **Preble Grille** for a deft Mediterranean take on local seafood and steaks and chops.

Day Two

After breakfast, stop at **Sawyer's Market** for picnic fixings. (Or go before breakfast — they open at 5:30.) Then head to Acadia National Park. Most visitors hit the highlights in a driving tour of Park Loop Road, but you'll get more from a focused, in-depth look at the park through the excellent free

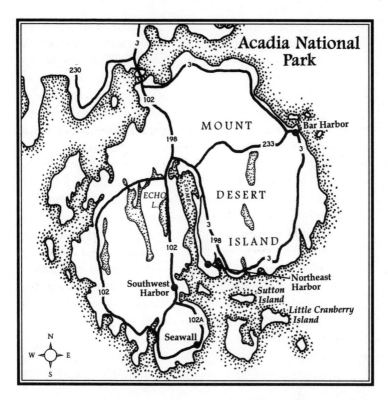

programs led by park rangers. One of the most frequent is the **Shoreline Discovery Walk,** a 2.5-hour, 1.3-mile exploration (moderate exertion) of natural attractions from forest to shore. It requires advance reservation (see "Essentials").

Within the eastern side of the park, you may also want to visit the **Wild Gardens of Acadia and the Abbe Museum** at Sieur de Monts Spring. The gardens reproduce 12 habitats of Mount Desert Island, each populated by typical wildflowers. The Abbe is devoted to Native American prehistory and, to a lesser extent, to history since European contact. Remember your haul this morning at Sawyer's? The spring is a fine spot for a picnic.

By now the park is getting crowded. (Peak usage is 10-2.) Hikers who wish to strike out on their own should ask for a brochure on Acadia's trails at the **Hulls Cove Visitor**

Center. The road network, a mix of 57 miles of carriage roads (now frequented by mountain bikers), was started in 1913 by John D. Rockefeller Jr. There are also well over 120 miles of hiking trails.

Another option is to explore a less-visited lobe of Acadia. Return to Southwest Harbor and pick up a mountain bike at **Southwest Cycle** to ride the Seawall Loop. Begin this easy ten-mile stretch by riding south from town on Route 102, following the signs toward the Swan's Island Ferry, which departs from the tiny but picturesque fishing village of Bass Harbor. A spur road leads down to Bass Harbor Light. Farther along the route, other turnouts offer exploring side trips to Ship Harbor Trail (a circular nature walk) and Wonderland Trails (an abandoned road that heads to a spectacular coast with pebble beach and myriad tidal pools). In short order you'll encounter the dramatic natural seawall with breathtaking ocean views. Three miles more and you're heading back to town.

The Seawall Loop passes within a few hundred yards of one possible dinner destination — **Keenan's.** A Louisiana-style roadhouse in Maine may seem odd, but consider that

---

THURSTON'S LOBSTER POUND

We all know that the best place to have lobster is at a lobster pound, and Thurston's in Bernard is one of a handful on Mount Desert Island. What makes this place so special is its simplicity and authenticity. It is located on a real working wharf, where we guarantee you a quintessential Maine experience. Picture this — you place your order at the window for clam chowder, corn on the cob, steamed lobster, and blueberry pie. You sit at a table that is right on the water in a "room" that looks as if somebody screened in the end of the dock. The light is fading, and in the pink glow of Bass Harbor fishing boats rock gently. You've never had fresher or sweeter lobster in your life.

Thurston's Lobster Pound, Steamboat Wharf Rd., Bernard. Open late May-September 11-8:30. 207-244-7600.

Long-billed curlew carved of basswood in 1979 by Wendell H. Gilley (1902–1983), one of 6,000 birds carved in his lifetime. (courtesy Wendell Gilley Museum)

this kind of establishment grows out of an abundance of seafood and a rural population. Besides, it's great food: baby back ribs, seafood gumbo, lobster. If you prefer a classic Maine experience, dine at **Beal's Lobster Pier** on fresh lobster, steamed clams, chowders. The picnic tables on the working dock are covered, in case a shower blows up.

Day Three

Pack up after breakfast, since you'll be heading out early to catch the **Nature and Island Lunch Cruise** from Northeast Harbor, which sails at 10. (Drive north on Route 102, then south on Route 198.) This 2.5-hour trip on the Islesford Ferry cruises past Bear Island Light and the seal and osprey habitats of Sutton Island before putting in at Little Cranberry Island. You can visit the Islesford Historical Museum and the tiny, quiet Catholic church down the road. If this is Sunday, enjoy brunch at the **Islesford Dock Restaurant** before the ferry returns at 12:45.

Back in Northeast Harbor, you might want to check the galleries and shops on Main Street before heading home. If you're feeling particularly expansive, a ring of polished beach stones set in 22k gold from **Shaw Contemporary Jewelry** would be a perfect souvenir.

– Patricia Harris and David Lyon

Essentials

Mount Desert Island Regional Visitors Center, Rte. 3. Open May to mid-October 9-8. 207-288-3411.

Acadia National Park, P.O. Box 177, Bar Harbor, ME 04609. 207-288-3338.

Victorian Inn at Southwest, Main St., Southwest Harbor. Double room with breakfast $90-$135. 207-244-3835.

Penury Hall Bed & Breakfast, Main St., Southwest Harbor. Double room with breakfast $65-$70. 207-244-7102.

Wendell Gilley Museum of Bird Carving, Main St. and Herrick Rd., Southwest Harbor. Open July-August Tuesday-Sunday 10-5; June and September Tuesday-Sunday 10-4. Adults $3, children 5-12 $1. 207-244-7555.

Echo Lake, Rte. 102, 4 miles north of Southwest Harbor.

Preble Grille, Clark Point Rd., Southwest Harbor. Open for dinner daily. $$-$$$. 207-244-3034.

Sawyer's Market, Main St., Southwest Harbor. Open Monday-Saturday 5:30 A.M.-6 P.M. 207-244-3315.

Shoreline Discovery Walk, Hulls Cove Visitor Center, Southwest Harbor. Open late May to mid-October daily. Free. 207-288-5262.

Wild Gardens of Acadia and the Abbe Museum, Sieur de Monts Spring, Bar Harbor. Open daily 9-5. Adults $2, children under 12 50¢. 207-288-3519.

Hulls Cove Visitor Center, Rte. 3 at Hulls Cove. 207-288-3338.

Southwest Cycle, Main St., Southwest Harbor. Open June-September Monday-Saturday 8:30-5:30, Sunday 10-4, $16 per day, including lock and helmet, reservation recommended. 207-244-5856.

Keenan's, Rte. 102A, Bass Harbor. Open for dinner daily 5-8. $-$$. 207-244-3403.

Beal's Lobster Pier, Clark Point Rd., Southwest Harbor. Open daily seasonally. $-$$$$. 800-245-7178, 207-244-7178.

Nature and Island Lunch Cruise, Northeast Harbor. Sails at 10 daily in season. Adults $11, children under 12 $7. 207-276-3717.

Islesford Dock Restaurant, 207-244-9455.

Shaw Contemporary Jewelry, 100 Main St., Northeast Harbor. Open in summer daily 9-7, off-season Monday-Saturday 9:30-5. 207-276-5000.

Day Trip: Kittery and York for Bargains and Beaches

MY FIRST HOME ON MAINE'S SOUTH COAST WAS A winter rental on Long Sands Beach in York. All that separated it from the surf was Route 1A, a skinny, desolate strip of road in winter, a ribbon of traffic, bikinis, and boom boxes in summer. When fierce winds brewed up a storm, town trucks sometimes plowed snow, but more often they plowed scattered stones back over the sea wall. Despite power outages and whistling clapboards (no wonder the rent was so reasonable), that winter forever bonded me to this coast.

I return to the area often, though I admit it is mostly in the summer and for short trips. My first stop is on Route 1 in Kittery for early morning, crowd-avoidance shopping at a few of the more than 120 outlet stores flanking the road.

The most scenic approach to the area is via Memorial Bridge on Route 1, a drawbridge connecting downtown Portsmouth, New Hampshire, to Kittery, Maine. If you get stuck on one side or the other while the bridge is up, get out of your car and walk toward the bridge for fine views — often you'll glimpse an international tanker entering the channel. It's an old bridge, thus a slow bridge, so don't worry about getting back to your car in time. You'll see the Portsmouth Naval Shipyard on Seavey Island to the east and the more hectic Interstate 95 bridge to the west. Continue north on Route 1.

Most of the Kittery outlets open at 9 A.M. during the week and 10 A.M. on weekends. I have my favorites, and I start at the northern end with the Reebok/Rockport store for deals on shoes and athletic gear and work my way south. There's Maidenform for bargain-priced undergarments, then I hit Chuck Roast Outerwear for rugged, New Hampshire-made fleece clothing. I never come to Kittery without stopping in at Kittery Trading Post, the Crate and Barrel outlet, and Liz Claiborne.

Since few have the stamina (or stupidity) to shop away a perfectly wonderful summer day, call ahead for a map of the outlets and plan your attack so you can be finished by noon. It's best to have a focused idea of what you're shopping for, but remember that some of the best bargains are the serendipitous ones.

By noon you should be back on the southern end of the strip. It's time for lunch — and the beach. Pick up a picnic of boiled lobsters, steamers, and cocktail shrimp at **Weathervane Seafoods.** This successful operation that now runs 18 restaurants got its start here at a humble little clam shack. But what the locals know is that around the corner from the main entrance is a small storefront for fresh fish purchases and take-out orders. The line is usually short or nonexistent, and they'll pack a lobster bake to go, no extra charge. Call ahead from your last shopping stop so lunch is bagged and ready when you get there.

Drive south to the Kittery traffic circle and follow signs for Route 103. You'll wind past historic homes and quiet coves. That's **Fort McClary** on your right just before Kittery Point. The fort was built in 1808 with additional construction in 1844 to 1886 and during the Civil War. Besides history, it offers sweeping ocean views.

But if your tummy can make it, drive a little father to Gerrish Island for a perfect picnic spot. After Kittery Point, take your first right past the gas station on the corner. There's a sign for **Chauncey Creek Lobster Pound,** which will be on your right. (This is another good choice for lobster-in-the rough. You're welcome to bring your own salad, bread, and spirits.) Your next right is over a small bridge. Follow the signs to **Fort Foster.** There's a small fee to drive in, but it's worth it. Sandy paths traverse the former fort, leading over grassy knolls, tree-shaded glens, and rocky shoreline. I drive out to Windsurfer's Beach and lug my picnic up a quick, steep path to a picnic table on the bluff. Time to break out the feast.

After lunch, stroll along the long pier (near the park's main parking lot) for a meditative moment, and watch the Asian families catching crabs for their dinner. The remains of an old house on an island close by are a reminder of a different century and way of life. There's a sandy area and playground for kids, but most children are happy poking in the rocks for snails and starfish and popping seaweed bubbles.

Back on Route 103, you'll thread through woodlands until the coast reappears as you cross the York River. At the intersection of Route 1A, York village lies just to your left; York Harbor and York Beach are to your right. There's only one actual town, but there are three separate and distinct localities: York village, with its white steeple and old New England charm; York Harbor, lined with grand historic homes; and nearby York Beach, the wild, fun-lovin' cousin.

Make a left and head into York village. York was first settled in 1624 and the **Old York Historical Society** does a fine job of preserving and promoting the town's past. Start your tour at the 1754 **Jefferd's Tavern Visitors Center** on the corner of Lindsay Road and York Street, just across from the burying ground. On an hour-and-a-half tour, you'll explore three centuries of maritime history, decorative arts, and architecture, including a schoolhouse, homes, a store, and the chilling Old Gaol (jailhouse); its cavernous cells date back to 1719. The diversity of the seven buildings and the spooky character of the jail work together to make this an interesting tour for children. Kids will also enjoy a ride on the **New England Trolley** that runs through York village, Harbor, and Beach. You can board the trolley at any one of 19 stops for a partial tour or remain onboard for an hour-long narrated tour.

By now it's early evening, the best time to meander up Route 1A along the shore. Take a right at the end of the beach onto Nubble Road, out past the many cottages that decorate the peninsula, to Sohier Park at the tip of Cape Neddick. From the parking area, you can view (and take a snapshot of) Nubble Light, the classic 1879 lighthouse perched on its own surf-beaten rock. Continue around the tip of the cape for a huge, homemade ice cream in any flavor imaginable at **Brown's Ice Cream.** For a taste of honky-tonk, stop in Short Sands, a Victorian-era seaside village with amusements, candlepin bowling, T-shirts galore, and saltwater taffy.

Finish the day with a touch of elegance. Continue on Route 1A north to Route 1, where at this intersection you'll see the **Cape Neddick Inn** on the left. Step inside and you will be transported — the windows are dressed in sheer drapes reminiscent of a Matisse painting, and you'll sip from hand-blown Italian stemware. Here you will find New American cuisine served with old-fashioned grace. Bunky plays the black baby grand, stirring the flames of the piano-top candelabra. Retreat to the lounge and sip rare brandy by the fieldstone fireplace, perhaps sharing chocolate ravioli smothered in berries and caramel, well-deserved luxury after a day of bargain hunting, beach bagging, and lessons in history.

– Carol Connare

E s s e n t i a l s

Maine Publicity Bureau/Kittery Information Center, Rte. 1 north or south and Rte. 95N. Here you'll find local and statewide travel information. 207-439-1319.

York Chamber of Commerce, P.O. Box 417, York, ME 03909. 207-363-4422.

Kittery Outlet Association, 888-458-8379.

Weathervane Seafoods, Rte. 1, Kittery. Open daily (except Thanksgiving) 11-9. For take-out call 207-439-0316, restaurant 207-439-0330.

Fort McClary, Rte. 103 on your right just before Kittery Point. Open Thursday-Tuesday 10-5. 207-439-2845.

Chauncey Creek Lobster Pound, Chauncey Creek Rd., Kittery Point. Open in summer only. 207-439-1030.

Fort Foster, Pocahontas Rd. (off Gerrish Island Lane), Kittery.

Old York Historical Society, Jefferd's Tavern Visitors Center. Open mid-May through September Tuesday-Saturday 10-5, Sunday 1-5. Adults $6, children $2.50, admission to one building $2. 207-363-4974.

New England Trolley starts on the hour at Dave's Thriftway on Long Sands Rd., York, and can be picked up at many locations including Jefferd's Tavern. Runs late June-Labor Day 10-8. Narrated tour $3, partial tour $1.50.

Brown's Ice Cream, Nubble Rd., York. Open seasonally. 207-363-4077.

Cape Neddick Inn, 1233 Rte. 1, Cape Neddick. Open in season daily 5:30-9:30, off-season Tuesday-Saturday 5:30-9:30. $$-$$$. 207-363-2899.

New Hampshire

For the Love of Portsmouth

OF ALL THE TOWNS IN NEW HAMPSHIRE, PORTSMOUTH extends the widest welcome. Every visitor finds something to love about it. Some would call Portsmouth a city (with a population of just under 25,000), but to me it has the character of a town: People exchange political views in front of the post office, and it's safe to stroll through the square at midnight. I lived and worked in Portsmouth for three years, and it will always hold a place in my heart.

Portsmouth's personality is shaped by its history. Its waterfront has been in constant use for over 350 years. Its deep, accessible harbor on the Piscataqua River gave rise to one of the earliest seaports in North America. The town today with its sparkling galleries, white-tablecloth restaurants, boutiques, and artisanal bakeries is a relatively new incarnation. I think of Portsmouth as an old coin rubbed shiny from much use.

Day One

Remember to pack your walking shoes. Portsmouth's charm is best experienced at sidewalk level, where you can stop to admire window boxes and storefronts. Once you park your car, you won't need it again until it's time to go home; everything is a short walk away.

Enter town at exit 7 off I-95. Take a right onto Market Street Extension and follow signs to the **Portsmouth**

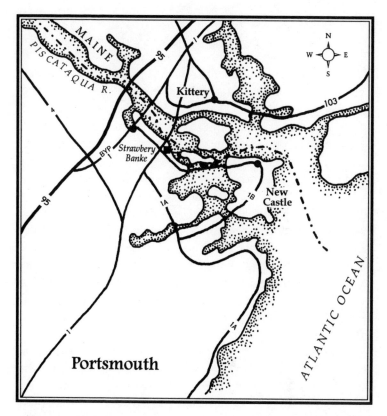

Chamber of Commerce on the right side of the road. Promptly buy a *Harbour Trail* guide and map. It's a wealth of information about Portsmouth history and a bargain at $2. Pick up a free *Guide to the Seacoast* too, with listings for lodging, dining, and shopping.

The finest place to stay is the **Sise Inn,** a restored 1881 Queen Anne-style mansion with 34 rooms, once the home of a wealthy Portsmouth merchant. (If you favor cozier quarters, try the no-smoking **Martin Hill Inn,** two 1800s houses separated by a brick courtyard offering four rooms and three suites.) Thread your car through the maze of skinny streets, taking a right onto Congress, a left onto Middle, then a right onto Court. Traffic usually creeps along in summer, just the right pace for people watching and following directions.

Stow your car and luggage at your inn, then set out on foot down Court Street to Pleasant Street. Head north to Market Square, the first stop on the Harbour Trail.

Since the mid-1700s the square has served as the civic hub of Portsmouth. In the 1700s it was the site of the meetinghouse, the statehouse for New Hampshire's Colonial legislature, and the site of military drills. There's a fair amount of marching here even today, bacause what was the first paved area of the city has become a bustling pedestrian plaza with the spire of North Church presiding over the hubbub.

The church's tall white spire is lit at night, providing a dramatic navigational landmark that you'll need as you wend your way through town. Notice a great deal of brick? North Church was one of many buildings constructed in the wake of two fires that leveled most of the town by 1806. And yes, that is a horse and buggy waiting near the church. Ray Parker's **Portsmouth Livery Company** offers 15- and 35-minute tours of town, the latter including a ride through Strawbery Banke.

Depending on your stamina, you can follow the sea-blue Harbour Trail signs to dozens of sites throughout the city. You will be enticed across the thresholds of many fine shops and eateries, but I urge you to resist — for now. Make a mental note and promise to return on Sunday to really shop.

I have a few favorite stops along the Harbour Trail. Be sure to find Ceres Street, named for the goddess of harvest. For 100 years, this waterfront avenue was the site of a farm market. Later it served as a ferry landing. Now the street is studded with eateries, shops, and the mooring site for Moran Tugboats. Look for the company's red and black tugs out on the water, guiding ships into port, where they'll unload industrial salts, fuel, and metals. Those are the piles you see when you first enter town.

At the corner of Bow Street is the **Dolphin Striker Restaurant** and its substreet level Spring Hill Tavern. A spring-fed well was discovered under the dining room during renovations in 1974; local historians verified it as the Spring Hill well, dating back to 1761. The bar was built around the well, which is covered by glass, providing an antiquated aquarium for a few well-heeled goldfish.

If you're hungry now, duck in at the **Ferry Landing,** a gritty local hangout near the tugboats. I always order the fried scallops — big, juicy, and never overcooked. But if you can wait, save your appetite for a full dinner in town later.

From Ceres Street, a short walk up Bow Street leads past **Porto Bello.** The aroma of garlic may tip you off. This Italian dining room sits two stories above the river, providing one of the best views of the waterfront. If you eat here, ask for a window table (there are only a few) so you can watch the harbor lights. The food is always fresh and authentic.

Farther up the hill is St. John's Church. Here America's oldest known working Brattle organ and a rare copy of the Vinegar Bible are housed. Keep the church on your right as you crest the hill to Harbour Place, a pretty brick mall near the Seacoast Repertory Theater. This, too, was a marketplace as well as a lumberyard and brewery. Follow a set of stairs down to the water's edge for a striking view of the harbor, Memorial Bridge (the earliest of Portsmouth's three bridges), and Kittery, Maine.

From here you can loop around to Prescott Park and Strawbery Banke, but I suggest you save that for tomorrow. Portsmouth's historic homes are also on the Harbour Trail, and each holds a surprise. The early 1700s Warner House has a lightning rod believed to be installed by Ben Franklin, as well as the earliest known painted murals in the United States. Make note of the Richard Jackson House. Built in 1664, it's the oldest house in the state.

After all this walking, you must be famished. The Sise Inn keeps a selection of local menus on hand. If you are a fan of sushi, indulge at **Sakura,** just south of the North Church in Market Square. You can sit at the sushi bar and watch as Japanese chefs deftly roll up sticky rice, sea vegetables, and fresh fish between bamboo mats, or ask to be seated in the sunken dining room with traditional low tables, no footwear allowed. Beyond all the delicious sushi and sashimi, I recommend the house salad with tangy ginger-carrot dressing, and the miso soup — the best I've ever had.

If you're not in the mood for Japanese, a good crowd-pleaser is the **Gaslight Grill** with its mouthwatering brick-oven pizzas downstairs and tasty grill fare upstairs. In summer there's an outdoor stage and bar behind the restaurant.

If you've energy to spare for a nightcap, stop back at the Spring Hill Tavern below the Dolphin Striker (look for all the local maritime art) or find the **Press Room.** It's the place with the old typewriter dangling above its door. An Irish-style pub, the Press Room features tap beer and lively music. Upstairs, pay a cover charge to hear prominent blues and folk musicians. You'll be humming all the way back to your room.

Day Two

Rise and shine for an early breakfast at **Karen's** restaurant on Daniel Street, because the line starts forming by 8:30 A.M. My favorite dish is French toast made from skyscraper slices of homemade cinnamon-raisin bread, but it has a flair for eggs dishes, too. Don't hold back, because today we tackle **Strawbery Banke,** an outdoor urban neighborhood history museum.

The tight cluster of historic houses and shops is named for the original waterfront neighborhood of Portsmouth. Four centuries of maritime history come to life here. Costumed interpreters and role-players act as members of families who once lived here.

As you stroll the grounds, visit with a working potter or boatbuilder. Chat with Governor Goodwin's wife on the porch of her mansion (ask about the detailed diaries she keeps on her garden), and talk to neighborhood children about their games. Off the kitchen of Abbott Store, a 1940s

At Strawbery Banke's Walsh House, Captain Walsh tells the story of his journey to trade New Hampshire lumber in the West Indies. (courtesy Strawbery Banke)

grocery, meet Nellie, who recounts the war effort and tells of her son who is a soldier.

I always visit the hopeful Pecunies Family Garden behind the Abbott Store; it's a 1945 Victory Garden laid out on its original site. One of my favorite houses is the Drisco House, with its contrasting restorations from the 1790s and the 1950s; on the kitchen table are boxes of Velveeta cheese and Tide in their early packaging.

You must pass through flowery **Prescott Park** to get to the waterfront, where the museum hosts special tours in summer. The 70-foot reproduction gundalow, the *Captain Edward H. Adams,* is moored here from May to September. Visit with the captain to learn how he drops the barge's mast to unload his cargo at the Sheafe Warehouse nearby. Inside the warehouse meet woodworkers crafting period boats.

Strawbery Banke recently unveiled its Shapiro House, the only single-standing Russian-Jewish immigrant house outside of New York City open to the public. Here you can visit with Shiva Shapiro, who may be cooking borscht with fresh beets from her garden. The year is 1919.

Such a vivid history lesson may have you coveting a piece of the past. Portsmouth is home to a number of antiques shops and secondhand stores, where you can find treasures to own. Just one block away from the museum is **Victory Antiques,** a group shop with a wide assortment of furniture, crystal, china, and special collections of trunks and brewery antiques. For a complete list of antiques stores, consult the chamber's free *Guide to the Seacoast.*

Tonight dine with the stars, both those overhead and those in the spotlight. Gather gourmet picnic treats at **Belle Peppers** before it closes at 6 P.M. In summer choose from a dozen deli salads; mix and match three for a dinner plate priced under five dollars. It also makes incredible sandwiches, and the gazpacho is unrivaled. With your blanket and picnic basket in tow, head for Prescott Park along the water. The blossom-covered grounds are the gift of two wealthy sisters who decided to beautify what had become, by the 1930s, an unsightly area of town. They bought up the tangle of decaying wharves, saloons, and bordellos and started planting. The park hosts an arts festival each July and August, featuring outdoor theater, music, and family shows.

Choose a picnic spot in front of the stage. If it's a weekend night, you'll be treated to a full-scale musical, beginning at 8 P.M. (Sunday shows start at 7 P.M.). After you've eaten, but before the show begins, leave your roost (your spot is secure as long as your blanket is there) and wander the pretty park. Peruse the beds of colorful annuals near the Liberty Pole. Experimental varieties of flowers are planted by University of New Hampshire horticulturists; the pole was first raised on this site in 1766 to protest the Stamp Act.

Day Three

Today is the day to act on all that window-shopping. Portsmouth has more stores than you'll ever be able to visit, so if you have a penchant for fine art or a love of jewelry, grab a *Guide to the Seacoast* so you can locate specialty sellers. For me the ideal shopping spree in Portsmouth begins at **Café Brioche** on the corner of Daniel and Pleasant streets, smack dab in Market Square. Modeled after a Parisian café, the grouping of wrought-iron tables on the sidewalk offers prime people-viewing.

If you need something different than coffee and pastry, check out the **Cyber Café,** one block south of the square. Here you can eat your breakfast (it has fresh-fruit smoothies) while surfing the Internet. Rent on-line time by the hour to send e-mails and faxes, print documents, and play computer games sitting at cherry-stained tables or on overstuffed couches.

My first stop is **Jari,** a store that resembles a sumptuous Victorian boudoir. Fine undergarments tumble from armoires, party dresses are draped over the English country couch, and hats are stacked on the bureaus. The dressing room is an 1801 vault from the first chartered bank in the United States.

I am a passionate cook and often fantasize about my dream kitchen. Bright ideas and products abound at **City & Country.** No more expensive than Crate and Barrel, the shop houses a distinctive collection of cookware, glassware, utensils, bath products, linens, and creative fixtures.

Within a few blocks of Market Square, you can find new-age medicinals, handmade chocolates, antiquarian books, home-brew goods, and kilim rugs. There are some classic stores on Market Street and Macro Polo for silly, inexpensive trinkets like pink flamingo salt and pepper shakers. At N. W. Barrett Gallery shop you'll find nifty — but never cute — crafts. The Paper Patch has the best cards in town and fine stationery, including a good selection of sealing wax and stamps.

Eventually you'll have to pull yourself away. When it's time to leave Portsmouth, take the long way. If you head southeast, you'll see signs for Route 1B. This leads to the island of New Castle, a charming settlement of beautiful old homes and fishermen's cottages, before rejoining Route 1. Follow the coastal route south for a final look at the sea.

— Carol Connare

Essentials

Portsmouth Chamber of Commerce, 500 Market St. Guided Harbour Trail tours offered in summer. 603-436-1118.

Sise Inn, 40 Court St. Double room with light breakfast buffet $99-$175. 603-433-1200.

Martin Hill Inn, 404 Islington St. Double room with full breakfast $70-$105. 603-436-2287.

Portsmouth Livery Company, 319 Lincoln Ave. 603-427-0044.

Dolphin Striker Restaurant, 25 Bow St. Open for lunch and dinner daily; Sunday brunch. $$-$$$. 603-431-5222.

Ferry Landing, Ceres St. Open mid-April through September daily 11 A.M.-11:30 P.M. $$. 603-431-5510.

Porto Bello, upstairs at 67 Bow St. Open Tuesday-Sunday 4:30-9:30. $$$. 603-431-2928.

Sakura, 40 Pleasant St. Open for lunch and dinner Tuesday-Saturday, dinner only on Sunday. $-$$$. 603-431-2721

Gaslight Grill, 64 Market St. Open for lunch and dinner daily. $. 603-430-9122.

Press Room, 77 Daniel St. Open for lunch and dinner Tuesday-Saturday, dinner only on Sunday. $. 603-431-5186.

Karen's, 105 Daniel St. Open for breakfast and lunch Monday-Friday 7-2:30, Saturday and Sunday 8-2:30. 603-431-1948.

Strawbery Banke Museum, Marcy St. Open mid-April through October. Candlelight strolls the first two weekends in December. 603-433-1100.

Prescott Park, Marcy St. Open year-round. Live entertainment July and August. Prescott Park Arts Festival information 603-436-2848.

Victory Antiques, 96 State St. Open Monday-Saturday 10-5, Sunday noon-6. 603-431-3046.

Belle Peppers, 41 Congress St. Open Monday-Friday 8-6, Saturday 9-6. $. 603-427-2504.

Café Brioche, 14 Market Sq. Open Sunday-Thursday 6:30-6, Friday-Saturday 6:30 A.M.-11 P.M. $. 430-9225.

Cyber Café, 75 Pleasant St. Open Monday-Saturday 9 A.M.-midnight, Sunday 11-8. $. 603-334-6638.

Jari, 26 Market Sq. Open Sunday noon-6, Monday-Thursday 10-6, Friday and Saturday 10-9. 603-427-6140.

City & Country, 50 Daniel St. Open daily 10-6. 603-433-5353.

A Ring Around Winnipesaukee

IN THE HEAT YOU'LL NOTICE THAT EVERYONE RUSHES to the water's edge, whether seaside or lakefront. This is no exception in the Lake Winnipesaukee area, but because the summer population here is mainly property owners and longtime family renters, even at the height of the season one can still find some peace. You'll discover that the country roads and small villages that make up what I've dubbed a "ring around Lake Winnipesaukee" are still blissfully unpeopled.

The "ring" starts at exit 18 from I-93, along the winding road that leads past the gazebo and general store of Canterbury Center to the hilltop **Canterbury Shaker Village.** A couple of hours spent touring these dignified white clapboard buildings and learning about the Shakers' religious beliefs and arts is fresh air for the mind. Plan your visit to coincide with lunchtime, and you can step inside the **Creamery Restaurant,** where chef Jeff Paige enlarges upon the basic Shaker recipes — cooling iced fruit drinks, wholesome sandwiches, and ginger ice cream. Picnic lovers might look for the signs for **Olde House Smoke House,** where sausage, turkey, rainbow trout, ham, and cheese are smoked and sold from an old stone smokehouse.

Rural roads in New Hampshire dip in and out of the past. Wend your way to Gilmanton, which comes on you suddenly with a cluster of clapboard houses and a brick mansion. Nestled in the village is the **Temperance Tavern,** now an inn with five guest rooms in a 1793 building.

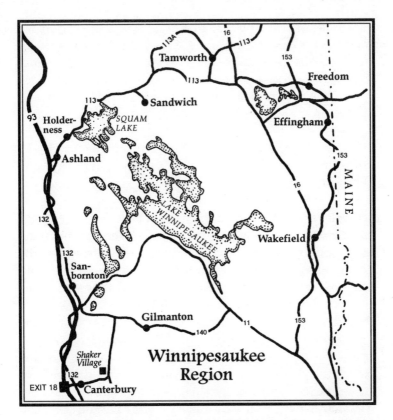

Anyone looking to skirt Lake Winnipesaukee in a hurry can jump back on I-93; but this trip isn't about speed, it's about poking. Therefore, follow the curves of older Route 132 as it weaves under the highway, through the 18th-century village of Sanbornton, and along the shores of Hermit Lake. When the road ends at Ashland, head east.

Holderness anchors an edge of Squam Lake, now permanently seared into our collective cinematic memory as Golden Pond. For a view of wild New Hampshire, stop at the **Science Center of New Hampshire.** It takes about an hour to wander the self-guided woodland Exhibit Trail, which winds past fenced habitats for bobcat, black bear, otter, and deer. You can also see wild turkeys up close (stunningly ugly creatures), as well as hawks, owls, vultures, and a bald eagle.

Route 113 can't be called a backbone of the region; it's more like a carapace. It splits off, attaches the letter A to itself, coexists with another route entirely, and sometimes goes in two directions at once. It's a two-lane dream back road through hardwoods and stands of pine. If you haven't dusted off the sports car for a while, this would be the place to do it.

Sandwich, a black-shuttered white clapboard classic, lies sandwiched between Lake Winnipesaukee and the White Mountains. In 1763 a group from Exeter petitioned the royal governor of the Province of New Hampshire for the right to settle a new town. Figuring a little fawning would stand them in good stead, they told the governor that if the land were granted, they planned to name the town after the governor's very good friend, the fourth Earl of Sandwich. The governor was flattered, the charter was granted, and the group had themselves a town more aptly named than they knew.

For the past hundred years, the **Corner House Inn** has served as a tavern in the center of Sandwich, and its Colonial-style dining rooms still make an excellent stop for lunch (order a bowl of the lobster-and-mushroom bisque). The **Sandwich Home Industries** and **League of New Hampshire Craftsmen** is a crafts-filled shop across the street, and there are a couple of antiques stores and other crafts shops in town to browse as well.

The **Sandwich Historical Society** is not too different from most other such small-town repositories: some furnishings, clothing from the 1800s and World War II, alien-looking cooking implements, and unwieldy farm tools. Early photographs of farmsteaders show stern expressions set in wrinkled and gaunt faces. The settlers' houses seem little more than lean-tos. Both are in contrast to the vigorous faces of today's inhabitants and their neatly restored 19th-century homes.

Gems are strewn along Route 113A, if you keep your eyes open for them: a granite fountain of clear spring drinking water; a marker denoting the site of Chinook Kennels, where the dogs for Admiral Byrd's first expedition to Antarctica were bred; the tiny Union Chapel at the bend of the road in Wonalancet. Much of this forest is second-growth; its ancestry, oaks and maples typically four feet in diameter, was cleared starting as soon as the settlers arrived in the 1700s. Using crude axes, the first farmsteaders may have taken three months to cut the timber on just one acre.

In the 1850s this area got its first taste of tourism when summer visitors began showing up. Tamworth village, like Sandwich, was disappointed that the railroad didn't build a local station. But it didn't take the two towns very long to discover that there was money to be made from the summer

---

WHERE JUD HALE TAKES HIS WIFE FOR DINNER

Jud Hale, longtime editor of *Yankee* Magazine and *The Old Farmer's Almanac*, considers Winnipesaukee his second home. He has spent summer weekends and vacations on an island here since 1971. The size of the lake, coupled with a good blend of peace (for Jud and his wife, Sally) and fun things to do (for the Hales' children and grandchildren), make the area a family favorite. Jud's first choice for dinner is the William Tell Inn. Every summer without fail he and Sally celebrate her July 10th birthday with dinner here. He says, "We always order the Wiener schnitzel, and it is always fantastic." For dessert the Hales' favorite is snowballs — two scoops of French vanilla ice cream rolled in toasted coconut with mounds of Swiss chocolate Tobler sauce. Vying for number 1 with snowballs is the Swiss Tobler cake. Owner-chef Peter Bossart and his wife, Susan, run the restaurant. He is Swiss, and his native meals are the most authentic you'll find outside of Switzerland. The cuisine is continental, and according to his wife, Peter also cooks the best filet mignon and rack of lamb anywhere. (Their Sunday brunch is known throughout the area, too.)

The William Tell Inn, Rte. 11, West Alton. Open Tuesday-Sunday 5-closing, Sunday brunch noon-3. Reservations welcomed. $$-$$$. 603-293-8803.

folk. Early on, these guests settled for most anywhere to stay and usually boarded at farmhouses. By the 1880s Tamworth had indulged in a few inns. The register of one included such notes as "Grand Oppera at Town Hall" and "4 men from Exeter caught 300 trout in 2 days."

Today the bigger draw in Tamworth is the **Barnstormers Summer Theatre,** which presents two summer months of plays. Carrying on the hospitality tradition is the **Tamworth Inn.** Phil and Kathy Bender are the perfect hosts at this big gray Victorian with 15 guest rooms, a dining room for traditional Yankee fare (look for chicken Tamworth), an outdoor pool, and a cozy pub.

Two steps down the street from the inn is the Barnstormers Playhouse; three steps and you're at Remick's Country Store and the Other Store, a pair of side-by-side general stores; three and a half steps put you in front of the Behr Farm, which sells vine-fresh produce. Four steps and you're out of town.

Almost 95 years ago, Sandwich alone claimed two dozen hotels and boardinghouses. Today there are barely half that many inns and B&Bs in the whole area. Among the small ones, the most unusual is **Red Horse Hill Farm,** where the owners can also stable your horse at their on-premises Morgan horse farm; **Highland House** is a meticulously restored 1790s Federal home originally built by a ship's captain, just outside Tamworth; and **Riverbend Inn** is a B&B that features breakfast views of the Chocorua River.

The best inn doesn't have any horses or a view of a river. It does have one of the best dining rooms in New England. **Staffords in the Field** is a big cream-colored farmhouse with a rocking-chair-bedecked veranda that sits high on a hill outside Tamworth. Guest rooms with modest antiques are found throughout the 1790s house, in an addition out back, as well as in three cottages. And from the inn's kitchen, Ramona Stafford serves simply perfect dinners. Everything, she says, should be perfect: from a silky chilled cucumber soup, a fresh herb vinaigrette on the salad, and chewy bread to the deboned and roasted duck or osso bucco. It sounds plain; it tastes spectacular.

Complete the circular route by heading way east to Route 153, which has a hard time deciding whether it's in New Hampshire or Maine. It doesn't matter: You'll drive through such tiny towns as Freedom, Effingham, and Wakefield. And on hot steamy weekends, chances are you'll hardly pass another car under the cool, leafy canopy along the way.

— Janice Brand

Essentials

Lakes Region Association, P.O. Box 589, Center Harbor, NH 03226. Ask here for numbers of chambers in surrounding towns. 888-925-2537, 603-253-8555.

Canterbury Shaker Village, Canterbury. Open April-October Monday-Saturday 10-5, Sunday noon-5; April, November, and December weekends 10-5. Tours are 90 minutes. Adults $9, children 6-16 $5. 603-783-9511.

Creamery Restaurant at Canterbury Shaker Village, Canterbury. Open May-October for lunch daily, for dinner weekends; 7 P.M. candlelight dinner Saturday, $34.50 including guided tour. Reservations required for dinner. Call for off-season hours. 603-783-9511.

Olde House Smoke House, 164 Briar Bush Rd., Canterbury. Open Monday-Saturday 10-5, Sunday noon-5. 603-783-4405.

Temperance Tavern, jct. rtes. 107 and 140, Gilmanton. Double room with breakfast $125 weekends, $85 Monday-Thursday. 603-267-7349.

Science Center of New Hampshire at Squam Lakes, Rte. 113, Holderness. Open May 1-November 1 daily 9:30-4:30. May, June, September, October adults $6, children 5-15 $3.50; July, August adults $8, children 5-15 $4; children under 5 free. 603-968-7194.

Corner House Inn, Center Sandwich. Double room with breakfast $80. Open for lunch and dinner June-October daily, November-May Wednesday-Sunday. $$-$$$. 800-501-6219, 603-284-6219.

Sandwich Home Industries and **League of New Hampshire Craftsmen,** 36 Main St., Center Sandwich. Open mid-May through mid-October Monday-Saturday 10-5, Sunday noon-5. 603-284-6831.

Sandwich Historical Society, 4 Maple St., Center Sandwich. Open June-September Tuesday-Saturday 11-5. 603-284-6269.

Barnstormers Summer Theatre, curtain time 8 P.M. For information write to P.O. Box 434, Tamworth, NH 03886. Call after July 3, 603-323-8500.

Tamworth Inn, Main St., Tamworth. Double room with breakfast $95-$140, with breakfast and dinner $120-$160. Open for dinner Tuesday-Saturday. $$-$$$. 800-NH-2-RELAX, 800-642-7352.

Red Horse Hill Farm, Bunker Hill Rd., South Tamworth. Double room with breakfast $70, no credit cards. 603-323-7275.

Highland House, Cleveland Hill Rd., Tamworth. Double room with breakfast $75. 603-323-7982.

Riverbend Inn, Rte. 16, Chocorua. Double room with breakfast $60-$135. 800-628-6944, 603-323-7440.

Staffords in the Field, off Rte. 113W, Chocorua. Double room with breakfast and dinner $120-$240. Open for dinner Tuesday-Saturday, $30 fixed price. 800-833-9509, 603-323-7766.

Pretty Villages and Antiques in the Upper Connecticut River Valley

THE NEW HAMPSHIRE SIDE OF THE CONNECTICUT RIVER valley from Westmoreland to Haverhill seems to have escaped the struggles of modern life. The small, prosperous towns inspire trust, the architecture is consistent and lovely, the traffic is negligible, and the pastimes are wholesome — flea marketing, antiquing, canoeing, fishing, bird-watching, walking, visiting auctions, and attending an occasional performance. Mostly unmarred by commercialism or industrialization, this route is almost entirely off the beaten path, passing by one major historic site and one prominent college town.

Day One
Begin your tour in early afternoon, driving west from Boston a little over two hours on Route 2 to Route 12, through Keene, New Hampshire. As you approach Westmoreland Depot, you will come over a rise for your first view of the Connecticut River, complete with meadows, cows, and a red

barn. Vermont, with its knobby hills worn down by the river and the retreating glacier 12,000 years ago, lies beyond. (From points south, pick up the drive at exit 3 on I-91. Take Route 9 east until you reach Route 63, where you'll turn north to meet Route 12 at the red barn.)

Drive north from Westmoreland Depot about five miles, turning right for a short side trip to Walpole. The hometown of Ken Burns, filmmaker of PBS's *Civil War* and other series, Walpole is the first of some of the prettiest villages along this itinerary. Among the pristine white clapboard houses and small shops on Main Street, don't miss **Burdick Chocolates** under modest brown-and-white striped awnings. Here you'll find the chocolate rated number one by *Consumer Reports.* Swiss-trained Larry Burdick forms delicate centers of flavor — ganache whipped with raspberries, ginger, fresh local cream, a hint of clove — then enrobes the morsels with Valrhona chocolate from France. Pull up a chair, sip some cappuccino or real hot chocolate (the kind made with steamed milk and shaved Valrhona) and take your time deciding what to take home.

Drive back to Route 12 and proceed north for a rural half hour to Charlestown. Reserve ahead of time for your first night at Joan DeBrine's cheerful B&B, **Maple Hedge,** an 1800 Federal-style house that is part of the National Historic District on Charlestown's main street.

In Charlestown, the northernmost British settlement during the 1740s, you can visit the **Fort at No. 4,** a reproduction of the fort the settlers established to protect themselves from the French-backed Indians, worth an hour's visit before it closes at 4 P.M. Or visit the **Foundation for Biblical Research,** a nonsectarian library and conference center, next door to Maple Hedge. The opulence of this large mansion hints at the sophistication and prosperity of the Connecticut River towns in early days. At least take a walk around town, which also happens to be baseball star Carlton Fisk's hometown.

Only a few restaurants exist nearby. You won't go hungry at **Indian Shutters,** just north of the town center and on the right — the food is basic New England fare. Don't miss the popovers, which are very good, and order the haddock, lobster, or steak.

Day Two

If today is Saturday, you begin with a choice: wait for the sumptuous breakfast served at Maple Hedge or join Eloise Savi and her dozen or so compatriots as they set off on their regular weekend birding jaunt, which meets in front of the Charlestown Library at 8 A.M. (weather permitting).

Whether it's breakfast or birds, afterward drive north on Route 12, turning left onto Route 12A about five miles out of town, bypassing Claremont to continue your indulgence in pastoral scenery, picturesque villages, and covered bridges.

About 25 minutes

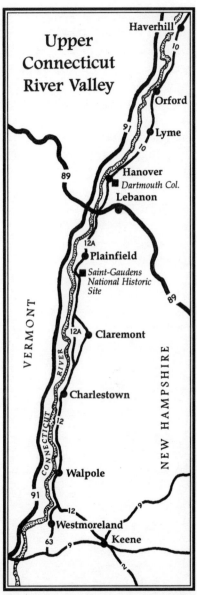

along the river will take you to the **Saint-Gaudens National Historic Site.** Augustus Saint-Gaudens sculpted many of the statues of politicians and military leaders that grace Boston,

New York, and Chicago public spaces. His home, studio, and gardens, all in a stunning mountaintop setting, became the center of an early 20th-century cultural colony and have been preserved. Plan to spend about two hours; if you're visiting on Sunday, there are concerts at 2 P.M.

Depending on when you plan to leave Saint-Gaudens, you may want to bring a picnic and enjoy the lawn's sweeping views. If not, continue on to Hanover for a late lunch.

To get to Hanover, take Route 12A north for about half an hour. Just before you reach I-89, you'll drive over a hill and be assaulted for about two miles by West Lebanon's visual cacophony of fast-food outlets, shopping malls, and traffic. Mercifully, Hanover soon appears. Wade through the traffic, following the signs to Route 10 north. Eventually you'll drive into downtown Hanover.

Hanover is the home of Dartmouth College, which keeps it a vibrant cultural gem. Lunch can be had at any of the inexpensive restaurants along South Main Street. Try **Lou's** for old-style shakes and burgers or the eclectic and cheerful **Molly's Balloon.** Light fare at either is less than $7.

Then spend a couple of hours touring the campus or

WHAT THE LOCALS KNOW

BEST GENERAL STORE IN AMERICA

Right over the river from Hanover, you'll find the best general store in America — Dan and Whit's in Norwich, Vermont. According to one of the owners, Jack Fraser, the store stocks around a quarter of a million items (the average hardware store has from 25,000 to 35,000, counting every type of nut and bolt). Here is just a sampling of their goods and services: barn jackets, boots, paints, excellent selection of wine, lawnmowers, shovels, posthole diggers, come-alongs, feed for every imaginable domestic animal, glass cutting, key making, and anything else you'd ever want, including free air for your car tires.

Dan and Whit's, Main St., Norwich, Vt. Open daily 7 A.M.-9 P.M. 802-649-1602.

*Costumed interpreters at the
Fort at No. 4 show us what
life was like in 1747, when the
British defended this northernmost settlement from attacking
French and Indian warriors.*
(courtesy Fort at No. 4)

visiting the **Hood Museum of Art** in the Hopkins Center.
The museum is noted for its splendid collection of Assyrian
reliefs from an 800 B.C. palace in what is now northern Iraq.
But its New Hampshire paintings and wonderful antique
furniture are equally pleasing. You might also find the Big
Apple Circus, a film festival, or a summer repertory performance at the Hopkins Center.

Considering Hanover's appeal, it is surprising to find
so few bed-and-breakfasts in the town itself. The somewhat
sterile and expensive **Hanover Inn** is certainly well located.
A few motels line Route 10 north. But the best idea for lodging is to drive north about seven miles to **Two Mile Farm,**
where you can enjoy Bud and Barbara Munson's 1790s New
England house and the peaceful countryside once again.
Reserve well ahead because Two Mile Farm has only three
rooms. Another choice is the 1809 **Alden Country Inn** in
Lyme, ten miles north of Hanover, a carefully restored building that has been an inn since 1918 and also serves dinner.

If you are in the mood for an elegant dining experience,
try the **Home Hill Country Inn,** a circa 1820s mansion in
Plainfield, 20 minutes south of Hanover. Chef Victoria du

Roure, who trained at the Ritz Hotel in Paris, prepares specialties such as foie gras with roasted garlic, veal sweetbreads sautéed with caramelized thyme onions, fresh spinach, and morels, and Maine lobster served out of the shell with truffles and champagne sauce.

Day Three

Today is devoted to architecture and antiquing. After breakfast, stock up for a picnic at the **Lyme Country Store,** since the New Hampshire towns north of Lyme have few restaurants. It has a large range of deli items and sandwiches, plus cheeses, maple syrup, and wine.

The first destination will be Orford. To get there, head out of Lyme west toward the Connecticut River. Turn right onto River Road just before the bridge, and you'll immediately feel you've stepped into a previous century. After about four miles, you'll cross a covered bridge and wind your way up to Route 10 north again, where seven-tenths of a mile later on the left you'll come upon Reed's Marsh, an old oxbow of the river that's a bird-watcher's haven.

Orford is just up the road. It's hard to understand why this remote village should have such an impressive collection of mansions. It's the setting — high on a ridge across from the dark palisades of Vermont — that took the fancy of the village's small-factory owners and merchants who, according to unverified legend, hired the prominent Boston architect Asher Benjamin to design houses worthy of North Country squires. The famous seven Ridge Houses are not open to the public, but they are impressive, even from the road.

If you're in Haverhill on the last Sunday of the month, you'll want to stop at the flea market on the common. Picnic on the lush grass of the common before you head back. Boston and Montreal are both about three hours away, and New York is less than five hours by Route 91 on the other side of the river.   – *Karen Cord Taylor*

Essentials

Hanover Chamber of Commerce, P.O. Box 505, 216 Nugget Building, South Main St., Hanover, NH 03755. 603-643-3115.

Burdick Chocolates, Main St., Walpole. Open Monday-Friday 8-6, Saturday-Sunday 9-5. 800-229-2419, 603-756-3701.

Maple Hedge, Main St., Charlestown. Double room with breakfast $85-$100. 603-826-5237.

Fort at No. 4, Rte. 12, Charlestown. 603-826-5700.

Foundation for Biblical Research, Main St., Charlestown. Open Monday-Friday 10-4. Free. 603-826-7751.

Indian Shutters, 149 Wheeler Rand Rd., Charlestown. Open Tuesday-Sunday 11:30-2 and 5-9, Saturday 5-9, Sunday 11:30-2:30. $$. 603-826-4366.

Saint-Gaudens National Historic Site, Rte. 12A, Cornish. Open Memorial Day-October daily 9-4:30. Adults $4, seniors and children free, guided tour on tape rental $1. 603-675-2175.

Lou's, 30 South Main St., Hanover. Open for lunch daily. $. 603-643-3321.

Molly's Balloon, 43 South Main St., Hanover. Open for lunch daily. $. 603-643-2570.

Hood Museum of Art, Hopkins Center, Dartmouth College, Hanover. Open Tuesday-Saturday 10-5, Thursday 10-9, Sunday noon-5. 603-646-2422.

Hanover Inn, on the Dartmouth Green, Hanover. Double room $217. 800-443-7024.

Two Mile Farm, 2 Ferson Rd., Hanover. Double room with breakfast $75-$90. 603-643-6472.

Alden Country Inn, 1 Market St., Lyme. Double room with breakfast $105-$160. Dinner nightly 5:30-9:30. $$. 603-795-2222.

Home Hill Country Inn & French Restaurant, River Rd., Plainfield. From Hanover exit 20 off I-89, to Rte. 12A south, right on River Rd., 3 miles ahead on the left. 603-675-6165.

Lyme Country Store, Rte. 10, Lyme. Open daily 6 A.M.-9 P.M. 603-795-2213.

Big Outlets and Big Outdoors in North Conway and Jackson

THERE ARE TWO KINDS OF SHOPPERS. WILLING PARTICIPANTS (WPs) look forward to a trip to the mall. They can tune out the Muzak, sobbing children, and traffic because they get high combing through the racks for bargains. Reluctant Purchasers (RPs) shop because they must. They broke a heel on the last pair of pumps, and no amount of dry cleaning will make that threadbare overcoat look new. RPs grit their teeth and pray for a good buy.

This trip has something for both breeds. RPs can storm the North Conway outlet stores one day and escape outdoors the next. WPs can spend both days snaking along Route 16 questing for deals in the outlets. Although some outlets appear to sell lesser-quality goods or regular merchandise at "sale" prices one could get at home, some bargains do exist. And you'll probably rub shoulders with hordes of Canadians, for whom any price break is a bargain.

The ideal time for this excursion to North Conway and Jackson is midweek, when crowds are smaller and some inns offer discounts. Before you go, contact the **Mount**

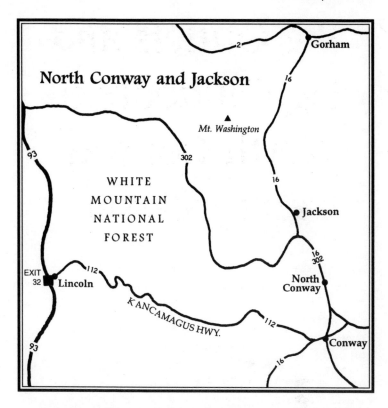

Washington Valley Chamber of Commerce for the *Official Guide to Mount Washington Valley.* It's full of ads but has an indispensable map of the outlets. It also suggests scenic hikes and walks.

Day One

Getting to North Conway is easy, but the route is indirect. From the south take I-93 north to exit 32 in Lincoln, and head east on Route 112, the Kancamagus Highway, a.k.a. the "Kank."

The Kank can be stop-and-go, but if you have the patience, it's worth the time: The 34-mile scenic byway cuts through the middle of the White Mountain National Forest.

There are several overlooks and great picnic spots. At Rocky Gorge Scenic area, about 26 miles east, a bridge over the loud falls leads to a footpath around Falls Pond.

Stop at the Saco Ranger Station at the eastern terminus of the highway, and pick up a one-page bulletin on moose watching — and avoiding. Moose are prolific, so be wary while driving in the White Mountains at dawn, dusk, or at night.

At the junction of routes 112 and 16, head north on 16 through Conway and then North Conway (noting your favorite stores on the map). Continue north to Route 16A and your base camp at Jackson.

This tiny resort town is a winter cross-country ski mecca. Lodging choices include two buildings designed by Stanford White. The **Inn at Thorn Hill** has a big front porch for rest and relaxation, a tiny pub, and a comfortable sitting room. Just down the street, the more basic **Inn at Jackson** offers big rooms and breakfasts to match. Across the way, the **Wentworth Resort Hotel** has no-nonsense rooms and offers golf and other packages. If you think you'll have cash left after your shopping spree, opt for an old-fashioned alpine experience at the **Nestlenook Farm on the River.** Situated on 65 acres, the 200-year-old building was renovated in

---

THE ONLY CUFF LINK MUSEUM IN THE WORLD

A quirky, fun new museum has just opened in the Yield House Industries Complex (their furniture and kits are a favorite with us). It is a cuff link museum with no fewer than 40,000 pairs from around the world! The cuff links belong to Claude Jeanloz, a vice president at Yield House, who started collecting more than 20 years ago. In addition to seeing some of the finest examples of cuff links anywhere, you can buy reproductions here as well.

The Cuff Link Museum, Yield House Industries, 71 Hobbs St., Conway. Open Monday-Friday 9-4. 603-447-8500.

Victorian gingerbread style. The hosts offer a wine and cheese bar for their guests.

You won't starve in Jackson. The Inn at Thorn Hill serves such entrées as ginger-cured pork tenderloin with cranberry chutney. The Wentworth serves American gourmet cuisine, and at **Wildcat Inn and Tavern** you can order hefty portions of lasagna, steak, seafood, or chicken.

Day Two

Most North Conway outlets don't open until ten o'clock, so have a leisurely breakfast. Although most true outlets are just south of North Conway village, a few Main Street shops are worth checking.

The **League of New Hampshire Craftsmen,** 0.3 mile south of the Conway Scenic Railway, offers high-quality crafts. Across the street at the Handcrafters' Barn, is **A Taste of New England,** where you can stock up on regional specialties: smoked meat, salsa, cookies, flours, preserves, horseradish, etc.

After you've warmed up with some preliminary shopping, continue south on Route 16/302. There are too many stores to mention, but here's a sample, moving north to south:

Danskin, Jonathan's Golf, Vermont Teddy Bear, Casual Corner, Corning Revere, and to revive you, Rocky Mountain Chocolate Factory. Farther south Dansk takes off as much as 60 percent on dinnerware, napkins, stemware, and cookware. The L.L. Bean Outlet Center includes some stores not listed on the chamber of commerce map, including a Joan & David outlet. L.L. Bean and Joan & David both discount some merchandise as much as 60 percent. At Cole Hahn, though, 50 percent off a $275 pair of shoes is still no bargain for us. RPs should avoid, at all costs, DKNY and Anne Klein, both at the L.L. Bean center. They're viciously expensive. (WPs will want to check them out anyway.)

After a full day of outlet hopping (and a fast-food

lunch), you may want to return to Jackson for a little down-time before dinner. Or for a change of scenery, stop in Glen (between North Conway and Jackson), and try the Bernerhof — which is now two restaurants, **Prince Place** and the **Black Bear Pub** — for fondues, Wiener schnitzel, and a chat with the friendly wait staff.

If you're traveling with children (who have been required to be patient while you shop), it is now their turn to have some fun. In Glen you'll find two family attractions — **Heritage New Hampshire,** a 300-year review of the state's past, and **Story Land,** a theme park with rides based on favorite children's stories.

It is no wonder Story Land is a perennial family favorite with its fairy-tale rides, petting zoo, gift shop, and restaurant.
(courtesy Story Land)

Day Three

RPs and WPs alike should get some morning exercise with a low-impact hike up Mount Willard. (If it's Sunday, stores don't open until noon anyway.) The trailhead is 3.5 miles west of the Wiley House on Route 302. The well-worn, modestly graded path takes about an hour to the summit in street shoes. And according to the *AMC White Mountain Guide,* "No other spot in the White Mountains affords so grand a view . . . for so little effort."

In the afternoon, hit the malls or go north on Route 16 to Mount Washington. From this side, the eastern slope, there are two ways up the 6,319-foot monolith, the Northeast's highest peak. If you've ever sneered at a "This Car Climbed Mt. Washington" bumper sticker, you've never driven the mountain. It can be nerve-racking: The **Mount Washington Auto Road** isn't paved the entire way; it's steep and has several hairpin turns. That odor on the way down is your brakes begging for mercy. Cars with automatic transmissions that won't shift into first gear aren't permitted up the auto road.

We like the **Guided "Stagecoach" Rides** across from the toll-road entrance in Gorham. You ride up the auto road in a van (equipped with heavy-duty brakes and gearing), while the driver cracks jokes and dispenses Mount Washington trivia. On a clear day the summit view (a half-hour stopover) includes the Atlantic Ocean off the Maine coast; Stowe, Vermont; and the Adirondacks.

From either Gorham or Jackson, retrace your route south to the Kancamagus then I-93.

– Lori Baird

Essentials

Mount Washington Valley Chamber of Commerce, Rte. 16, P.O. Box 2300-G, North Conway, NH 03860. 800-367-3364, 603-356-3171.

Inn at Thorn Hill, Thorn Hill Rd., Jackson. Double room with breakfast and dinner $160-$300. Dinner nightly 6-9. $$$. 800-289-8990, 603-383-4242.

Inn at Jackson, Thorn Hill Rd., Jackson. Double room with breakfast $69-$159. 800-289-8600, 603-383-4321.

Wentworth Resort Hotel, Rte. 16A, Jackson. Double room $99-$179; higher rates include breakfast and dinner. Dinner nightly 6-9. $$-$$$. 800-637-0013.

Nestlenook Farm on the River, Dinsmore Rd., Jackson. Double room with breakfast $125-$230. 800-659-9443, 603-383-8071.

Wildcat Inn and Tavern, Rte. 16A, Jackson. Open for dinner Sunday-Thursday 6-9, Friday and Saturday 6-10. $$-$$$$. 603-383-4245.

League of New Hampshire Craftsmen, Rte. 16, North Conway. Open daily 10-5. 603-356-2441.

A Taste of New England, Rte. 16, North Conway. Open Sunday-Thursday 9-5, Friday and Saturday 9-6. 603-356-8996.

Prince Place at the Bernerhof, Rte. 302, Glen. Dinner nightly 5:30-9:30. $$$. 603-383-4414.

Black Bear Pub at the Bernerhof, Rte. 302, Glen. Serving all afternoon and evening until 10. $. 603-383-4414.

Heritage New Hampshire, Rte. 16, Glen. Open mid-June to Labor Day 9-6. Call for off-season hours. Adults $7, children $4.50, under 4 free. 603-383-9776.

Story Land, Rte. 16, Glen. Open mid-June to Labor Day 9-6, weekends in the fall 10-5. Admission, $12 for all ages includes all rides. 603-383-4293.

Mount Washington Auto Road, Gorham. Open mid-May to mid-October daily 7:30-6. $15 for car and driver, adults $6, children 5-12 $4, includes souvenir cassette of scenic tour. 603-466-3988, 603-466-2222.

Guided "Stagecoach" Rides, Gorham. Open mid-May to mid-October daily 8:30-5. Adults $20, children $10. 603-466-3988, 603-466-2222.

Autumn in the North Country

IF YOU'RE WILLING TO ABIDE A SOMETIMES SPOOKY remoteness and a decided lack of tourist amenities, the North Country serves up autumn at its purest and most unadulterated. The dense forests seem to challenge the hilly farmsteads for supremacy rather than to accept peace. At the meadow's edge, brilliant maples and saffron birches contrast with the dark, austere spires of spruce.

This remote boreal region, well north of most White Mountains attractions, is characterized by low mountains and large meals, most of which are served at restaurants with little prospect of a review in *Gourmet*. With the notable exception of the Balsams, tourist services tend to be sparse and more rough-hewn. But for those searching for an autumn far from the outlets and crowds, the North Country is hard to beat. Begin in Bethlehem.

Day One

One option is the **Mulburn Inn,** a seven-room B&B located just east of town on Route 302. This 1913 cottage was originally built as a retreat for a Woolworth heir and has since been updated. The James Madison Room is in a turret, and the inn features maple floors and stained-glass windows. Our favorite in Bethlehem is the **Adair,** a country estate on 200 acres with views of the Presidential and Dalton ranges. The three-story mansion was built in 1927 by nationally

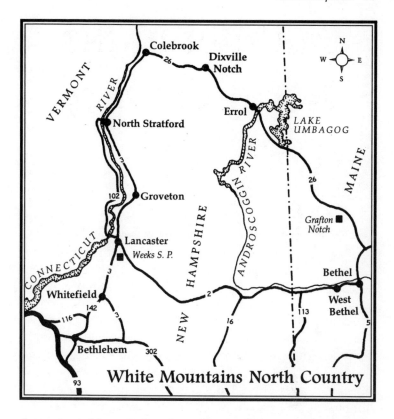

White Mountains North Country

famous trial lawyer Frank Hogan for his daughter Dorothy as a wedding gift. The house, lived in and loved by Dorothy Hogan Guider for 64 years until her death in 1991, retains all the qualities of a gracious home. In the early 1990s Hardy and Patricia Banfield and their daughter Nancy transformed the house into a luxury country inn. From April to November the restaurant Tim-Ber Alley offers excellent food in the Adair's dining room.

Once settled, take a sunset stroll along the gentle trails at the **Rocks,** a magnificent estate of meadows, woodlands, and shingled barns now managed by the Society for the Protection of New Hampshire Forests. The well-marked entrance is two miles west of Bethlehem on Route 302. Each year approximately 7,000 new Christmas trees are planted

The Adair, pictured here in the winter, is a year-round favorite among its guests. (courtesy the Adair)

here for a total of nearly 1,600 trees per acre. If more vigorous hiking is your pleasure, head for the White Mountain National Forest **Ammonoosuc Ranger Station** on Trudeau Road off Route 302 for information.

For dinner, **Lloyd Hills,** within walking distance of the Mulburn, offers simple pub fare amid stamped tin ceilings and a relaxed ambience.

Day Two

After breakfast, set out on winding Route 142 north to Route 116, which shortly connects with busy Route 3. Heading north, you'll soon pass through the many-spired town of Whitefield, situated around an irregular green in a stately river valley.

Between Whitefield and Lancaster you'll come upon the entrance to Weeks State Park. Turn here and ascend the narrow 1.5-mile paved drive to the top of Mount Prospect (elevation 2,059) for a stunning look at the North Country. There's a handsome stone fire tower next to the former manor house of John W. Weeks, a onetime U.S. Secretary of War. Sturdy steps take you to an arcaded lookout atop the tower, where you'll find superb views of the Presidential Range and the northern mountains of New Hampshire and Vermont. A manned fire lookout is located above the arcade; visitors are welcome at the ranger's discretion.

Continuing northward toward Lancaster and Groveton, Route 3 becomes somewhat more commercial. A pleasant alternative is to cross the bridge into Vermont and follow twisting Route 102 along the west side of the Connecticut River. Recross the river back to New Hampshire at North Stratford.

Heading east on Route 26, away from the Connecticut River, you'll soon arrive at the legendary **Balsams,** one of the few grand resorts that has survived the automobile and the motel. The Balsams caters primarily to conventions in the fall, with a limited program for individual travelers, but it still makes an appealing autumn destination.

This sprawling resort, which first opened in 1866, is situated on 15,000 rugged acres and maintains a number of superb hiking trails. Check in early enough to allow exploration of the grounds and a game of golf or tennis.

For budget-minded travelers, there's **Mohawk Cottages,** just outside Colebrook on Route 26. Five clean but spartan two-bedroom cottages feature kitchenettes and fireplaces. Spend the afternoon exploring the Connecticut Lakes region to the north, or head to the **Colebrook Fish Hatchery** just east of town on Fish Hatchery Road. This former state facility offers fly-fishing for brown, rainbow, and brook trout at a private pond (no license required). Release your catch, or pay by the inch and enjoy fresh trout for dinner at your cottage.

Day Three

After breakfast, continue eastward on Route 26. Past Dixville Notch the road unfolds through rolling hills, past waterfalls, and over rivers. In the one-horse town of Errol, stop at the **Errol Restaurant** for one of its famous homemade dough-nuts, then try to make it last long enough to enjoy it while lounging at the bridge over the Androscoggin River on the east edge of town. On most weekends you're liable to find kayakers or canoeists daring the rapids on this challenging stretch of river.

Continue up the hill toward Maine. Keep an eye over your left shoulder for some good views of Lake Umbagog straddling the state border, but also be alert for moose in the road. Soon you'll arrive at Grafton Notch, a dramatic glacial valley. The drive through here is extraordinary, but to really appreciate autumn, take a few breaks to explore by foot.

Mother Walker Falls, so marked on a roadside sign, takes some snooping to uncover; it's a small cascade hidden beneath a massive boulder that long ago crashed to the val-ley floor from the mountains above. At Screw Auger Falls, just off the highway, the river courses through a steep, kinked gorge. For a more remote set of cascades, hike the half-mile up to beautiful Step Falls, where a stream has carved arcs and pools down a smooth granite face. To find the falls, which are owned by the Nature Conservancy, drive a mile or so past Screw Auger Falls until you cross a cement bridge over Wright Brook. Immediately turn left on an unmarked dirt road into a field and park beneath the pines at the far edge. A registration box and map are located in the woods just off the parking area.

In the bustling town of Bethel, Maine, there's a good choice of hotels and motels, many of which cater to the ski crowd at Sunday River. The best bet for outdoor enthusiasts is the rustic **Telemark Inn,** located at the end of a dirt road several miles outside Bethel. Owner Steve Crone specializes in guided llama hikes and uses this Adirondack-style 1900 retreat as a base. Sign up for a full- or half-day llama trek, or head out on your own. Steve can suggest hiking trails in the newly created Caribou-Speckled Wilderness Area.

– Wayne Curtis

Essentials

Bethlehem Chamber of Commerce, P.O. Box 748, Bethlehem, NH 03547. 603-869-2151.

Northern White Mountains Chamber of Commerce, 164 Main St., P.O. Box 298, Berlin, NH 03570. 800-992-7480, 603-752-6060.

North Country Chamber of Commerce, Box 1, Colebrook, NH 03576. 603-237-8939.

Mulburn Inn, 2370 Main St., Bethlehem. Double room with breakfast $65-$90. 603-869-3389.

The Adair, 80 Guider Lane, Bethlehem. Double room with full breakfast $135-$220. 888-444-2600, 603-444-2600.

The Rocks, Rte. 302, Bethlehem. 603-444-6228.

Ammonoosuc Ranger Station, off Rte. 302. Open Monday-Friday 7-4. 603-869-2626.

Lloyd Hills, 2061 Main St., Bethlehem. Dinner nightly 5-9. $$. 603-869-2141.

The Balsams, Rte. 26, Dixville Notch. Open mid-May to mid-October and mid-December through March. Double room with all meals and activities $248-$410. 800-255-0600, in New Hampshire 800-255-0800.

Mohawk Cottages, Rte. 26, Colebrook. Double room $55. 603-237-4310.

Colebrook Fish Hatchery, Fish Hatchery Rd. 603-237-4459.

Errol Restaurant, Errol. Open daily at 5 A.M. $. 603-482-3852.

Telemark Inn, RFD 2, Bethel. Double room with breakfast $90. 207-836-2703.

Day Trip: A View from Mount Monadnock

I HAVE LIVED IN THE MONADNOCK REGION FOR NEARLY 20 years. It is my home and I consider myself a local. This south-central part of New Hampshire encompasses about 40 towns. In my migration around the area over the years, I have lived in seven of these. Each town has its place in my memory. I recall the logging road in Hancock where I saw my first moose, the coffee shop in Peterborough where I set eyes on my husband, the little cemetery in Jaffrey Center with Willa Cather's grave tucked in the corner, and the old Cape in Greenfield where we brought our daughter home after she was born. From these towns I, too, recall the best view of the mountain that gives the region its name. In my time there have been many, many changes — in life and in the surrounding towns — but Mount Monadnock stays the same. For many of us who live here, Monadnock is the constant, an anchor. Though we don't get up the mountain as often as we'd like, it is the place we take visitors to first. When I return from a trip from any direction, I know exactly where I will get my first glimpse of Monadnock. Then I know I am home.

Imagine you are an old friend and you have come to visit. Our perfect Monadnock day begins with a hike.

Because I am a local, I have consulted our resident expert, Larry Davis. He has hiked to the summit for more than 2,000 consecutive days (that's five and a half years, if you're counting). Monadnock is the most-hiked mountain in the world, but even on Columbus Day weekend when better than 12,000 people head up, Davis says you can find a spot for yourself. His advice is to avoid the White Dot Trail and head instead up the Parker Trail to the Lost Farm Trail (you'll see it in about ten minutes). Ask for a map of the hiking trails at **Monadnock State Park.** On a clear day you can see both the Boston skyline and Mount Washington from Monadnock's 3,165-foot summit. The most appealing thing about hiking here is that we get above tree line so swiftly and for much of the time we are on a "moonscape" with unfettered views. We've reached the summit, and we've lucked into one of those rare crystalline days where all six New England states are visible. Like Davis, tap the geological survey marker with your boot and take a long look.

The only thing better than the view is coming down knowing that after an hour's effort a delicious lunch awaits. With appetites fully justified, we're ready for Peterborough. Downtown, in an area called Depot Square, there has been a reawakening. The train ran through here years ago, and after serving as a town parking lot, Depot Square is once again the center of activity. New stores have set up shop and old ones have gotten a face-lift. **Twelve Pine,** long a favorite of mine, has opened up new quarters here, offering everything from sandwiches to salads, pastas, pizzas with homemade crust, and its all-time-popular chicken burritos. Proprietors Danny and Joan Thibeault are what I call "food people." They know quality ingredients and have excellent cooking skills plus the good sense to avoid being trendy or fussy. Twelve Pine has delicious prepared foods to eat there or take home, fresh juices, fine coffees, the best-looking produce outside your own garden, gourmet items, fresh flowers, and an assortment of health foods. I guarantee you will not be able to

Mount Monadnock — on a clear day you can see the Boston skyline and Mount Washington from its 3,165-foot summit. (photo by Arthur Boufford, courtesy Mount Monadnock State Park)

avoid buying more than you can eat, even if you did just hike Monadnock. Consider this a blessing; just take the leftovers home for dinner.

Across the parking lot stop at the **Sharon Arts Center** for one of the largest selections of quality handcrafts in the state. The galleries and studios for the Sharon Arts Center are located on Route 123 in Sharon, where classes and workshops are offered. Just recently it has moved its extensive inventory to Depot Square. When I have a wedding present to buy, I go to either the Sharon Arts Center or the **North Gallery at Tewksbury's,** located at the corner of routes 101 and 123. The only year I didn't do the bulk of my Christmas shopping at the North Gallery was when it closed after a fire. The owners rebuilt the barn, and now it is jam-packed with crafts, cookbooks, jewelry, prints, toys, ornaments, soaps, kitchen items, and a loft with antiques and discounted merchandise. A bonus: free gift wrapping for picture-perfect presents.

Some other of my favorite shops in Peterborough are **At Wit's End** on Grove Street and around the corner on Main Street **Joseph's Coat,** where you'll find unique gifts from every continent, fabrics of the highest quality, and magic dresses, so called because they can be worn in 50 different ways. The **Black Swan** on Route 101 sells handcrafts, soaps, candles, dried flowers, and other gift items. For book browsing, don't miss the **Toadstool Bookshop,** where titles number 45,000, with another 5,000 used and out-of-print books upstairs. The children's section is the most thorough I've seen; as far as I'm considered, you'll not find a better bookstore around.

The Monadnock region is a cultural gem. For its size, it has an inordinate number of nationally known writers, painters, photographers, illustrators, and craft workers. Peterborough is home to the MacDowell Colony, founded in 1908 to give writers, artists, and musicians a refuge from everyday worries so they can work. It is here that Thornton Wilder wrote the play *Our Town.* Peterborough likes to claim *Our Town,* but the truth is that many other Monadnock towns served as inspiration as well. Years before Wilder, other writers like Henry David Thoreau and Ralph Waldo Emerson mused about Monadnock — the mountain, that is. At the turn of the century Dublin became known as a cultural center, attracting writers Mark Twain and Willa Cather and artists Abbot Thayer, Frank Benson, and Rockwell Kent.

Not all my friends want to start the day with a strenuous hike. Fortunately for all of us, you won't find a better place for a slow scenic ride in the car. Here is my "Sunday drive" through a handful of the prettiest towns: Hancock, just north of Peterborough on Route 123, has a quarter-mile main street where nearly every house is listed on the National Register of Historic Places. In the meetinghouse Paul Revere's bell #236 chimes the hour. A few houses down

Main Street, the Hancock Inn has been in continuous operation since 1789, visited by thousands, from cattle drovers and
rum runners to aristocracy and presidents. Across from
Norway Pond is one of my favorite cemeteries. A few years
back my aunt and cousin were visiting, and we spent a long
time reading stones here. After much chatting and calling to
one another to see this epitaph or unusual name, we found
ourselves standing quietly before a tall, ornate marble stone.
On it was engraved two names and the figure of a woman
lying in a bed holding a tiny baby. I have never taken a visitor to this stone who has not said a silent prayer.

From Hancock take Route 137 south, and in a little over
three miles look for Hancock Road on your right. This will
take you past Lake Skatutakee and into the tiny town of
Harrisville. This is perhaps my favorite of all. Here tidy brick
buildings and a large granite mill are strung along the mill-
stream that once powered a woolen mill. On the hill sits a
long boardinghouse. The buildings are fully restored, thanks
to a savvy nonprofit group that leases them out to various
businesses, including the internationally known Harrisville
Designs, makers of looms and yarns for handweavers and
knitters. If you turn right at Harrisville Designs and cross the
bridge, you'll find a group of five millworkers' houses called
"Peanut Row." Beyond these is Sunset Beach, the town's private little beach and a nice spot for a picnic. Harrisville is the
village most painted by artists (even more than Hancock)
and is one of the oldest existing textile communities in the
country. One Harrisville resident told me that the town's
authenticity lies in the fact that it is still a working community. As she puts it, "Living in Harrisville is like being able to
have dinner every night in Colonial Williamsburg."

Backtrack through Harrisville, but instead of taking the
road around Skatutakee, take Dublin Road to Route 101.
Turn right here (toward Marlborough) and take a left on
Upper Jaffrey Road. In about seven miles this road ends.
Turn left heading east on 124 to Jaffrey Center. This town is
more spread out than either of the previous small villages

and so has a grander feel. The large, steepled 1773 meeting-house presides. Behind here is another of my favorite cemeteries, the old burying ground. You won't have to nose around this one to find a specific grave site, because there is a map posted on the horse sheds. I always go first to Willa Cather's and read the quote, "… That is happiness; to be dissolved into something complete and great," from *My Antonía,* then to Amos Fortune's. He was an African slave who bought his freedom and at his death left money to the church. A renowned summer lecture series held here is named after him. Like all choice towns in the Monadnock Region, this one has water. Take Thorndike Pond Road for about a mile and a half, and on your left the woods open to a stunning view of the mountain over the water. Access here is not public; the town landing is on the west side of the lake, so just take in the view.

If you're not making dinner of the leftovers from Twelve Pine, try **Del Rossi's Trattoria** on Route 137 in Dublin. The pasta is always fresh and cooked to order. Live bluegrass and folk music play nearly every Saturday night. In Peterborough the best choice is **Latacarta,** where chef Hiroshi Hayashi prepares delicious meals with natural ingredients. Carnivore and vegetarian alike will find something that pleases.

After dinner, drive to Dublin Lake on Route 101 for a last look at the mountain. In the summer you can do no better than this twilight view. Linger to watch the shadow of the western ridge move across the hollow of the mountain as the sun sets. *– Polly Bannister*

E s s e n t i a l s

Monadnock Travel Council, 315 Washington St., P.O. Box 358, Keene 03431. 800-432-7864, 603-355-8155. (It has a very good guide to the region.)

Greater Peterborough Chamber of Commerce, 10B Wilton Rd., P.O. Box 401, Peterborough 03458. 603-924-7234.

Monadnock State Park, off Rte. 124, Jaffrey. Ages 12 and up $2.50. Strictly no pets allowed. 603-532-8862.

Twelve Pine, Depot Square, Peterborough. Monday-Friday 8-7, Saturday and Sunday 9-4, closed holidays. 603-924-6140.

Sharon Arts Center, Depot Square, Peterborough. Monday-Saturday 10-5, Sunday noon-5. 603-924-2787.

North Gallery at Tewksbury's, Rte. 101, Peterborough. Monday-Friday 10-6, Saturday and Sunday 10-5. 603-924-3224.

At Wit's End, Grove St., Peterborough. Monday-Saturday 10-5:30, Sunday 11-4. 603-924-9115.

Joseph's Coat, 26 Main St., Peterborough. Monday-Saturday 10-6, Sunday 11-5. 603-924-6683.

Black Swan, 107 Wilton Rd. (Rte. 101), Peterborough. Open daily 10-5. 603-924-7906.

Toadstool Bookshop, Depot Square, Peterborough. Monday-Friday 10-6, Saturday 10-5, Sunday 10-4. 603-924-3543.

Del Rossi's Trattoria, Rte. 137, Dublin. Monday-Thursday 5-8:30 P.M., Friday and Saturday 5-9, Sunday 4-8 P.M. 603-563-7195.

Latacarta, Noone Falls Mill, Rte. 202 South, Peterborough. Open Monday-Saturday 5-8:30 P.M. 603-924-6878.

Vermont

Snow-Covered Countryside, Hearty Dinners, and Chocolate

IT HAS BEEN MANY YEARS SINCE I HAVE GONE DOWNHILL skiing, and the truth is, I don't miss it much. My favorite things about this popular winter pastime were seeing the snow-covered countryside, eating chocolate, and enjoying big dinners. Then it occurred to me: I can do all those things and I don't have to freeze on the lift. What a revelation. Here is an itinerary for three wonderful days not skiing in southern Vermont.

Day One
There are more than two dozen inns and B&Bs in the Manchester area of southern Vermont. This is a pricey neck of the woods, and you don't always get your money's worth. Paying $155 (plus seven percent sales tax plus, often, a 15 percent service charge) for a room in a motel that calls itself an inn is not my idea of a good deal. The following I do recommend.

For budget, there's the nine-room **Ira Allen House** in

Arlington. Its prices are the best, its decor home-style func-
tional. The five-room **Seth Warner Inn,** on the Arlington side
of Manchester, is a tidy Colonial with stenciled walls and
four-poster beds. Somewhat pricier is the highly recom-
mended **Inn on Covered Bridge Green** in West Arlington.
With only five rooms, it was Norman Rockwell's home and
studio from 1943 to 1954. Don't expect originals on the walls,
says the innkeeper, "It was a matter of owning one of his
works or owning the property."

Here are some other places that are in my view worth
their price. The **West Mountain Inn** in Arlington is consistently rated one of Vermont's most popular inns (see "What
the Locals Know" to find out more). At the **1811 House** in the
center of Manchester, the building is Colonial style, but the

*The view from the West Mountain Inn is always dramatic — in
autumn color, snow, or spring blossom. (courtesy West Mountain Inn)*

accents are all elegant English. The grande dame of
Manchester village is the **Equinox Hotel,** a true resort with
on-premises health spa, indoor-outdoor pool, golf course,
choice of restaurants, and valet parking. The **Inn at Ormsby
Hill,** owned by Ted and Chris Sprague, on Route 7A south of

the village, has ten rooms, all with fireplaces and two-person Jacuzzis. The innkeepers serve a Friday night "supper," at $20 per couple, of soup or pasta or stew with homemade bread and dessert. Saturday night, Chris dons her chef's toque again for elegant four-course dinners ($65 per couple). Meals are served only to inn guests.

Settled in? Good. Now eat. If you're staying elsewhere than Ormsby Hill, try the **Black Swan,** a handsome brick Federal sitting above Route 7A in Manchester and serving French-accented continental fare. In the Equinox the **Marsh Tavern** offers a light menu in a cozy setting of dark walls, tartan carpet, and fireplace glow.

Day Two

Now that you're already here, you will need a little orienta-tion — there are three different Manchesters. Manchester Depot, at the intersection of routes 11/30 and 7A, has become Vermont's Freeport with outlets of such names as Giorgio Armani, Donna Karan, and Anne Klein. Depending on your tolerance for bargain hunting and shopping, you'll be either enthralled or disgusted. I'm both at once.

Manchester village is the quiet and elegant neighbor-hood of marble sidewalks strung along Route 7A at a safe remove south of the shopping frenzy. Here you'll find the Orvis Store (look in the basement for discounts) and the **American Museum of Fly-Fishing.** With displays of rods and reels and videos featuring fish that seem never to get caught, it's a mecca for all fisherfolk. In the row of shops across from the Equinox is **Frog Hollow, the Vermont State Craft Center.** Equinox guests get a ten percent discount, something to consider if you fall in love with an $1,800 hand-crafted cherry table.

But Manchester Center captured my fancy. Flanking Route 7A just north of the intersection with routes 11/30, this was once a separate town known as Factory Point. Its 19th-century buildings now house crafts stores and small restaurants.

Spend the morning in whichever Manchester appeals most, or head south on Route 7A to **Hildene,** the summer estate of Abraham Lincoln's son, Robert Todd Lincoln. The house is closed in winter, but you can cross-country ski the grounds' groomed trails. Aim for Manchester Center for lunch. If you got your innkeeper up early (most outlets and even Orvis open at 9 A.M.), there's no harm in a second breakfast of sourdough pancakes at **Up for Breakfast.** Since it was reviewed in *Gourmet,* you can now expect lines on weekends. Locals have lunch at the **Gourmet Deli Café,** housed in a former barn in the Green Mountain Village Shops complex just north of Up for Breakfast. Look for the brochure called *Historic Main Street Shopping* for a nicely written history of Manchester Center.

Then head south on Route 7A to Arlington, specifically **East Arlington Antique Centers,** with a combined 12,000 square feet of stuff. I promised chocolate on this trip: On 7A in Shaftsbury, look for the **Chocolate Barn,** a mecca for chocoholics with its molds and handmade truffles, clusters, jellies, patties, mints, and fudge in milk, dark, and white chocolate, plus two floors of antiques.

If you have time, continue into Bennington, turning left on Route 76A, then right on West Main Street to the **Bennington Museum.** Here you'll find an interesting assortment: Civil War uniforms, flintlock rifles, a 1925 touring car, and an outstanding array of American glass. The museum is especially noted for its exceptional collection of Bennington Pottery, including 4,000 pieces of Rockingham Flint Enamel. The museum also displays the largest public collection of paintings by Grandma Moses and the one-room schoolhouse she attended as a child.

I have no problem spending money on a swell dinner tonight; the way I look at it, I saved $100 today on a pair of lift tickets. The **Arlington Inn** has fireside tables, with chef Thomas D'Olivio offering a continental menu. The local heavyweight is **Chantecleer.** The Equinox joins the running with its **Colonnade,** very fancy, very expensive, and open only on weekends and then only when not booked by a private party.

Day Three

Explore the southern Vermont hills that haven't been carved up by skiers. Head east on routes 11/30, then turn north on Route 11. Take the left turn into Peru, which starred as Hadleyville in the Diane Keaton movie, *Baby Boom*. In the upstairs studio of **Miller Woodcarving** is the "Hadleyville" sign Miller carved, as well as the other whimsical things he does with wood. **J. J. Hapgood General Store,** built in 1827,

THE BEST PLACE FOR A REAL VERMONT WEDDING

Anyone who has ever stayed at the West Mountain Inn in Arlington understands why this cozy place runs at 70% occupancy rate in an industry where 20% is considered average. But what a lot of people don't know is that the West Mountain Inn is where Michael J. Fox got married. Long before his wedding, though, many brides had selected this inn for their happy day. West Mountain innkeepers Wes and Mary Ann Carlson and their longtime staff make guests feel relaxed and nurtured without interfering. The only time fussing comes into play is when manager Paula Maynard is planning a wedding, something she does quite devotedly about ten times a year. "We recognize that each couple have a vision of their wedding," says Paula, "and we make that come to life." You won't find a prettier spot for saying your vows than this hilltop converted summer home that overlooks the Battenkill. The West Mountain Inn has something for everyone (not just brides). Here you'll find walking and cross-country ski trails, llamas, a baby sitter so you can enjoy the gourmet meals in peace, and a gift of an African violet to take home. Don't forget to ask at the front desk for a copy of its Vermont shopping tour called, "Norman's Loop."

West Mountain Inn, located ½ mile west of Arlington village on Rte. 313. Double room with full breakfast and dinner $186-$224. 802-375-6516.

is an old-fashioned country grocery with wood floors that slope precipitously.

Continue on Route 11 to Londonderry, turning south on Route 100, then picking up Route 30 again. Stop for a muffin in Jamaica at the **Jamaica Coffeehouse,** which also sells maple syrup, crafts, clothing, and jewelry.

It's definitely worth a look around as you pass through Newfane, its famous courthouse and pair of white inns off to your right. It's another 17 miles into Brattleboro. Before hopping onto I-91 and points home, stop for a sandwich at the **Latchis Grille,** inside the art deco Latchis Hotel, where you might also sample from the on-site Windham Brewery. Reflect on what a lovely time you've had — and no one broke a leg.

– Janice Brand

E s s e n t i a l s

Manchester and the Mountains, Manchester Center, Manchester, VT 05255. 802-362-2100.

Arlington Chamber of Commerce, P.O. Box 245, Arlington, VT 05250. 802-375-2800.

Bennington Area Chamber of Commerce, Veterans Memorial Dr., Bennington, VT 05201. 802-447-3311.

Ira Allen House, Rte. 7A, Arlington. Double room with breakfast $80-$100. 802-362-2284.

Seth Warner Inn, Rte. 7A, Manchester. Double room with breakfast $90-$100. 802-362-3830.

Inn on Covered Bridge Green, Rte. 313 at the covered bridge, West Arlington. Double room with breakfast $110-$185. 800-726-9480, 802-375-9489.

1811 House, Rte. 7A, Manchester village. Double room with breakfast $110-$200. 800-432-1811, 802-362-1811.

Equinox Hotel, Rte. 7A, Manchester village. Double room with breakfast $169-$309, packages available. 800-362-4747, 802-362-4700.

Inn at Ormsby Hill, Rte. 7A, Manchester Center. Double room with breakfast $115-$260. Dinner Saturday for inn guests only. $$$$. 802-362-1163.

Black Swan, Rte. 7A, Manchester. $$-$$$. 802-362-3807.

Marsh Tavern at the Equinox Hotel, Rte. 7A, Manchester village. Dinner nightly. $-$$$. 802-362-3807.

American Museum of Fly-Fishing, Rte. 7A, Manchester village. Open every day 10-4. Adults $3. 802-362-3300.

Frog Hollow, the Vermont State Craft Center, Rte. 7A, Manchester village. Open Monday-Saturday 10-6, Sunday 10-5. 802-362-3321.

Hildene, Rte. 7A, Manchester village. Closed in winter. 802-362-1788.

Up for Breakfast, 710 Main St., Rte. 7A, Manchester Center. Open Monday-Friday 6-noon, Saturday and Sunday 7-1. 802-362-4204.

Gourmet Deli Café, Green Mountain Village Shops, Rte. 7A, Manchester Center. Open daily for lunch. 802-362-1254.

East Arlington Antique Centers, Rte. 7A, Arlington. Open daily 9-5. 802-375-6144, 802-375-9607.

Chocolate Barn, Rte. 7A, Shaftsbury. Open daily 9:30-5:30. 802-375-6928.

Bennington Museum, West Main St., Bennington. Open November 1-May 31 daily 9-5, June 1-October 31 daily 9-6. Adults $5, seniors and students $4.50, under 12 free. 802-447-1571.

Arlington Inn, Rte. 7A, Arlington. Open for dinner Tuesday-Saturday. $$$-$$$$. 800-443-9442, 802-375-6532.

Chantecleer, Rte. 7A N, Manchester. $$$-$$$$. 802-362-1616.

Colonnade at the Equinox, Rte. 7A, Manchester village. Open for dinner weekends only. $$$-$$$$. 800-362-4747.

Miller Woodcarving, Rte. 11, Peru. Open "most of the time, except when I'm out." 802-824-3077.

J. J. Hapgood General Store, Rte. 11, Peru. Open Monday-Saturday 8:30-6, Sunday 8:30-1. 802-824-5911.

Jamaica Coffeehouse, Rte. 30, Jamaica. Open daily 8-5, closed Tuesday. 802-874-7085.

Latchis Grille, 6 Flat St., Brattleboro. Open Tuesday-Friday 5:30-9 P.M., Saturday and Sunday noon-10. $-$$$. 802-254-4747.

Three Days Exploring Covered Bridges and Back Roads

FEW IMAGES SAY "VERMONT" CLEARER THAN THOSE OF covered bridges. But why were the bridges covered? I've read that they were covered to keep snow and ice off the wooden planks so horses wouldn't slip. Another theory says that horses feared crossing water at a height; covering a bridge would fool the horse into thinking it was entering a barn. But the most plausible reason is plain old Yankee practicality — covering a bridge protects the structural members in the span. Periodic replacement of the roof is far simpler (and cheaper) than repairing the timbers below. Sensibility aside, we're the lucky heirs of one of New England's most picturesque images, and this itinerary packs in enough for you to go through a couple of rolls of film.

Day One

To make the most of your first day, plan to spend the night before in Woodstock. Lodging ranges from the deluxe **Woodstock Inn and Resort** to modestly priced motels such as the **Woodstock Motel** and **Shire Motel.** I stayed with my wife, Mary Ellen, and our two young children just outside

Woodstock at the **October Country Inn.** Only an eight-mile drive from Woodstock, the inn is on a quiet country road, far enough from the crowds that converge on Woodstock in the summer and fall.

Start the morning as we did: Mary Ellen set off to explore Woodstock's many shops, while I herded the children to the **Billings Farm and Museum,** a real working farm. Another kid-pleaser is the **Vermont Raptor Center.** This outdoor museum houses birds of 26 species; all the birds have permanent injuries that prevent them from being released back into the wild. Then head for the bridges. Follow Route 12 west for about a mile until you see the sign for South Pomfret. Turn right onto this back road into a countryside of pasture and forest. At South Pomfret bear right at the fork; in about four miles follow the signs for Sharon and I-89 by turning to the left. This road ends where it overlooks the White River in Sharon.

Take a left on Howe Hill Road and follow it for four miles to the beautiful common of South Royalton. The 1850 **South Royalton House,** owned and operated by Vermont Law School, makes a fine stop for salads, sandwiches, and a wide variety of other lunch choices. Covered bridges begin

---

TOUGH GLOVE

A visitor to Randolph would never know the Green Mountain Glove factory is there. Hidden away in the town's "industrial" section, with only a modest wooden sign over the front door, you'll find it. Since 1920 the Haupt family has been turning out wonderfully supple yet durable work gloves out of deer and goat skin. They are famous among utility linesmen and in the garden supply catalog Smith & Hawken for being the toughest gloves on the market. You can buy them right off the shelf at the factory, a converted creamery, and feel pretty smug because, as they say on TV, "they're not sold in stores."

Green Mountain Glove, Pearl St., Randolph. Open Monday-Friday 7-3. 802-728-9160.

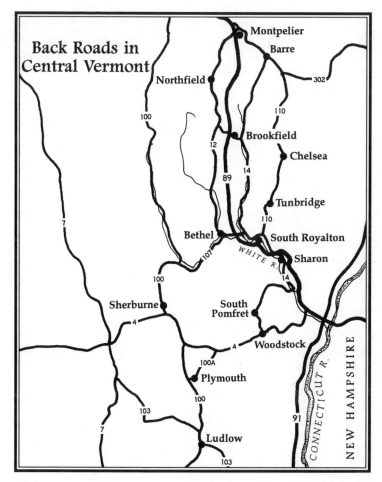

to appear with regularity as you leave South Royalton on Route 110 north to Tunbridge. The first one you pass is the Howe Bridge, built in 1879. When passing through Tunbridge, you can't help but notice the sign for the "World's Fair." Held annually in mid-September, it's an old-fashioned agricultural fair featuring such events as pony- and ox-pulling. Just beyond the Tunbridge Town Hall is the Mill Covered Bridge (1883), with this sign over the entrance: "One dollar fine for a person to drive a horse or other beast faster than a walk or drive more than one loaded team at the same time on this bridge." The Larkin Bridge and Moxley Bridge are alongside Route 110 farther to the north. In Chelsea take a moment to wander about the village's two greens. A hidden hamlet far off the beaten path, Chelsea seems untouched by time, and we loved its simplicity. For those who wish to spend more time here, the **Shire Inn,** a beautiful Federal-style home built in 1832, is just a few minutes' walk from the center of town.

Continue on Route 110 into Barre to visit the world's largest granite quarry, **Rock of Ages.** A 30-minute shuttle-bus tour takes you through the 115-year-old quarries, and you can view the manufacturing operations from an observation deck. At the nearby Hope Cemetery, about a mile and half north of Barre Common on Route 14, you can see the elaborate stone carvings crafted by Vermont's turn-of-the-century stonecutters. Montpelier (population 8,500), the smallest state capital in the nation, is just west of Barre on Route 302. It is compact enough to tour on foot, and there are many fine shops to explore. For lunch or dinner, try the **Main Street Grill and Bar,** operated by the New England Culinary Institute (also on the premises is Chef's Table, another showcase for NECI talent that features a prix-fixe menu built upon local ingredients such as lamb and farm-raised game). For overnighting, families could choose the **Capital Plaza Hotel** or the **Econo-Lodge.** Couples might prefer the **Inn at Montpelier,** a large 1828 Federal-style house with elegantly furnished rooms and period antiques.

Day Two

Dog River is just a couple of miles away, so trout-fishing enthusiasts may want to rise before the rest of the family and test their skills. I was on the river at dawn and managed to fool a fat brown trout, which I let go after photographing it. Late risers can tour the **Vermont State House** and take a seat in the gallery to watch the legislature, if it is in session. Nearby is the **Vermont Historical Society Museum,** where I

Exploring the countryside by horse offers just the right pace for taking in Vermont's scenery. (courtesy Vermont Tourism and Marketing)

was absolutely fascinated by the stuffed cougar — the last one shot in the state, in 1881.

There are many choices for lunch, but we enjoyed sandwiches from the **Country Store.** Then take Route 12 south into Northfield Falls. There are three covered bridges on Cox Brook Road, adjacent to the Falls General Store. The first two bridges are within sight of each other, making for a very interesting photo opportunity.

Seen enough covered bridges? How about a 320-foot-long bridge that floats on 380 barrels? To see the Floating Bridge at Brookfield, continue on Route 12 south exactly 5.3 miles from where it splits with Route 12A. A sign for the bridge will direct you to turn left on a back road; the bridge is about 3½ miles down at Sunset Lake. To continue the loop to the south, follow Route 65 east, then turn onto Route 14 south, a quiet back road passing farms, sleepy towns, and more covered bridges. Route 107 takes you southwest into Bethel. Stop for a tour at the **White River National Fish Hatchery.**

Follow Route 107 to Route 100 south, past the Giorgetti Covered Bridge and into the Sherburne-Plymouth-Ludlow area. Options for a night's lodging range from the basic **Farmbrook Motel** to the elegant **Governor's Inn.** We stayed at the **Hawk Inn and Mountain Resort,** where we had a choice of horseback riding, bicycling, or canoeing with our children. Rates vary widely depending on whether you stay at the inn or in a townhouse or mountain villa.

Day Three

Spend the morning as we did at Buttermilk Falls in Ludlow, a picturesque spot for picnicking or swimming; take the first right (Buttermilk Falls Road) off Route 103 after its intersection with Route 100. For a more action-packed morning try the **Pico Alpine Slide.** A good choice for lunch is the **Old Farmhouse Inn.** Devote the afternoon to history at the **President Calvin Coolidge State Historic Site,** where President Coolidge was born in a small house attached to a general store. At the nearby **Plymouth Cheese Factory** you can watch the cheese-making process, then purchase a wedge to snack on in the car while driving the 12 miles back to Woodstock.   *– Michael Tougias*

Essentials

Woodstock Area Chamber of Commerce, 18 Central St., P.O. Box 486, Woodstock, VT 05091. 802-457-3555.

Randolph Area Chamber of Commerce, 66 Central St., P.O. Box 9, Randolph, VT 05060. 802-728-9027.

Woodstock Inn and Resort, on the Green, Woodstock. Double room $159-$325. 800-448-7900.

Woodstock Motel, Rte. 4, Woodstock. Double room $40-$90. 802-457-2500.

Shire Motel, Rte. 4, Woodstock. Double room $68-$155. 802-457-2211.

October Country Inn, Bridgewater Corners. Double room with breakfast and dinner $124-$156, children 5-12 sharing room with parents $25, under 5 free. 802-672-3412.

Billings Farm and Museum, Rte. 12, Woodstock. Open May 1-October 31 daily 10-5. Adults $7, children $3.50. 802-457-2355.

Vermont Raptor Center, Church Hill Rd., off Rte. 4, Woodstock. Open May 1-October 31 daily 9-5, November 1-April 30 Monday-Saturday 10-4. Adults $5, children $2. 802-457-2779.

South Royalton House, on the Common, South Royalton. Open Monday-Friday 11:30-2. 802-763-8315.

Shire Inn, Chelsea. Double room with breakfast $90-$145, MAP also available. 802-685-3031.

Rock of Ages, 773 Graniteville Rd., Barre. Open mid-May through mid-October Monday-Friday 9:15-3. Adults $4, seniors $3.50, children $1.50. 802-476-3119.

Main Street Grill and Bar, 38 Elm St., Montpelier. Open daily for lunch and dinner. $-$$. 802-223-3188.

Capital Plaza Hotel, 100 State St., Montpelier. Double room $82-$102. 802-223-5252.

Econo-Lodge, Rte. 12, Montpelier. Double room $56-$85. 802-223-5258.

Inn at Montpelier, 147 Main St., Montpelier. Double room $99-$155. 802-223-2727.

Vermont State House, 11 South State St., Montpelier. Open Monday-Friday 8-4. 802-828-2228.

Vermont Historical Society Museum, 109 State St., Montpelier. Open Tuesday-Friday 9-4:30, Saturday 9-4, Sunday noon-4. Adults $3, seniors and students $2, children under 12 free. 802-828-2291.

Country Store, 82 Main St., Montpelier. Open daily 7 A.M.-9 P.M. 802-229-4284.

White River National Fish Hatchery, Rte. 107, Bethel. Open daily 8-3. 802-234-5241.

Farmbrook Motel, Rte. 100A, Plymouth. Double room $45-$65. 802-672-3621.

Governor's Inn, 86 Main St., Ludlow. Double room with breakfast $130-$170, children over 12 welcome. 802-228-8830.

Hawk Inn and Mountain Resort, Rte. 100, Plymouth. Double room $189-$279. 800-685-HAWK.

Pico Alpine Slide, Rte. 4, Sherburne. Open July 4-Labor Day daily 10-5, early season Memorial Day-July 3 weekends only 11-5, late season Labor Day-Columbus Day weekends only 11-5. Admission $4-$20, depending on number of rides and rider's age. 802-775-4346.

Old Farmhouse Inn, rtes. 103 and 100, Rutland. 802-228-8700.

President Calvin Coolidge State Historic Site, Rte. 100, Plymouth. Open May 23-October 18 daily 9:30-5. Adults $5, children under 14 free. 802-672-3773.

Plymouth Cheese Factory, Rte. 100A, Plymouth. Open daily 8-4:30. 802-672-3650.

Catching the Breeze in the Lake Champlain Islands

YOU'RE LYING ON A WHITE SAND BEACH UNDER A BLUE sky. Waves gently lap the shore, and sailboats and windsurfers catch the breeze. Now brace yourself for the surprise: You're in Vermont. Lake Champlain boasts some lovely, uncrowded beaches, and one of the best ways to sample them is on a trip to the Champlain islands. South and North Hero (named for Ethan and Ira Allen of Revolutionary War fame), Isle La Motte, and Alburg (actually a peninsula) — with their rolling hills, old barns, and weathered split-rail fences — have a soft, pastoral beauty that is the perfect foil to the rugged mountains looming on both sides.

Day One

Start your trip with an overnight in Burlington on the shores of Lake Champlain. A late afternoon arrival will allow you to explore the city's lively pedestrian mall, Church Street Marketplace. The Vermont State Craft Center recently opened a branch of its **Frog Hollow Gallery** here, and the state's best-known creation — Ben & Jerry's ice cream — is just a short stroll away at 36 Church St. For accommodations, the **Radisson Hotel Burlington** has unsurpassed views across the lake to the Adirondacks — be sure to request a lakeside room.

Downtown has many good restaurants. **Parima** is a new restaurant serving Thai cuisine. Small and lively is the **Daily Planet,** serving ethnic dishes like Caribbean duck, Thai chicken, and Greek seafood pasta. If you're in the mood for something sinful, try Ben Cohen and Jerry Greenfield's favorite spot, **Al's French Frys,** where you'll find fries by the quart, pint, and cup, hamburgers, hot dogs, and grilled chicken breast. It is always busy here, but the secret is that if all you're getting is fries, you can move to the head of the line. (For more local favorites, see "What the Locals Know.")

After dinner, head to the lake, where you can sit on swinging benches at Waterfront Park (base of College Street) and watch dusk envelop the mountains.

Day Two

Before leaving town, you may want to pick up food for a picnic lunch. For one-stop shopping, the **Fresh Market Cheese Outlet** has gourmet foods, cheeses, and wines; and across the street is **Lake Champlain Chocolates.** Or visit **Mirabelles,** a European-style bakery and café that would also make a fine breakfast stop. Follow Main Street over the hill and take I-89 north to exit 17 (Route 2 west). Just before the causeway to the islands is **Sand Bar State Park,** where you can swim in the warm, shallow water, walk the wide, sandy beach, rent a boat, or sit and gaze over to the islands.

Once on South Hero, Route 2 winds past villages, orchards, and old fields with thick stands of cedar. The islands are small and low, so one is never far from the water.

On a calm day Lake Champlain is sparkling and inviting. You can catch a short ferry ride from Grand Isle (the town at the north end of South Hero island) to Plattsburgh, New York, at the **Lake Champlain Transportation Company.** Next to the ferry terminal is the state's new multimillion-dollar fish hatchery, the **Grand Isle Fish**

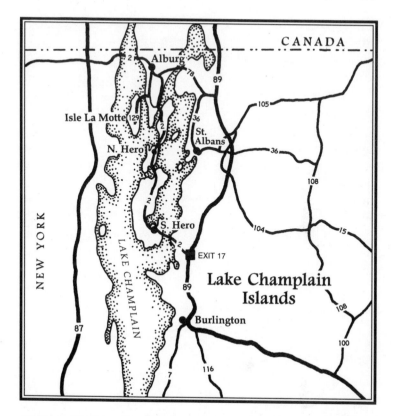

CANADA

2 Alburg
78
89
105
Isle La Motte 129
36
2
St.
Albans
N. Hero
36
108
2
104
15
S. Hero
2
EXIT 17
89
Lake Champlain
Islands
108
Burlington
100
87
7
116

NEW YORK

LAKE CHAMPLAIN

Culture Station. Its visitor center is open daily, with a self-guided tour, aquaria, and displays on the ecology of the lake. Back on Route 2, stop north of Grand Isle village at the **Hyde Log Cabin.** Built by Jedediah Hyde in 1783 of hand-hewn cedar logs, it may be the oldest log cabin in the country — no one's disproved the claim.

If you've packed a picnic lunch, cross the drawbridge to North Hero and **Knight Point State Park,** where in 1830 John Knight opened his ferry service between the two islands (the original landing can still be seen). Or if you're feeling adventurous, you can rent a boat from **Tudhope Sailing Center and Marina** and head to **Knight Island State Park,** a lovely undeveloped island crisscrossed by trails. Otherwise, catch a budget lunch at one of the clam stands

North Hero is the summer home of the Royal Lipizzan Stallions of Austria. (courtesy Lake Champlain Chamber of Commerce)

along Route 2, or take in the views from the wood-paneled dining room at **Shore Acres,** a sprawling, secluded resort that offers 23 lakeside rooms and big lawns that slope gently to the water. While in North Hero, take a stroll around the village, a state historic district. The county courthouse, built in 1824, has stone walls 2½ feet thick and fine woodwork inside. The **Island Craft Shop** is a co-op that features work by regional artisans; it's located behind **Hero's Welcome,** an "upscale country store," featuring gourmet groceries, unusual gifts, and the Lake Store, offering everything you might need on the water. Every summer North Hero hosts the **Royal Lipizzan Stallions of Austria** (July 9-August 30, 1998).

The islands abound with affordable lodgings. One of the nicest is the **Thomas Mott B&B,** a restored 1838 inn. The five rooms all have private baths, handmade quilts, and gorgeous lake views. Owner Pat Schallert, a former professional wine taster, invites his guests to use his canoes and sailboat and to help themselves to the Ben & Jerry's, always stocked in the freezer. On North Hero you'll feel like a child visiting your grandparents at **Northland B&B.** Maybe it's the old-fashioned wallpaper or the feel of a house that's been in the same family for three generations (owner Charlie Clark was born downstairs). Elsewhere on the islands, **Paradise Bay B&B** has three spacious rooms in a modern

---

BEST EATS IN THE BURLINGTON AREA

Deborah Straw has lived in Burlington since 1972, and for the past several years she has been a local restaurant reviewer. Here are a few of her favorites.

The Blue Seal. From its Caesar salad with roasted red peppers to its vegetable quesadilla or pan-roasted salmon, this is a restaurant where fresh produce and innovation matter. Situated in a granary built in 1854 in downtown Richmond, this is the perfect spot for a romantic, leisurely dinner. Bridge St., Richmond. Open Tuesday-Saturday 5:30-9:30, Sunday during foliage season. $$. 802-434-5949.

Perry's Fish House. Awarded the best seafood restaurant in the area each year from 1993 to 1997 by the *Burlington Free Press* Readers' Poll, this is a large, festive eatery. The motif is nautical, the portions generous, the fish fresh, the service friendly, and there are lots of choices for landlubbers. 1080 Shelburne Rd., South Burlington. Open Sunday 4-10, Monday-Thursday 5-10, Friday-Saturday 4:30-11. $$-$$$. 802-862-1300.

Sweet Tomatoes. In a town with several Italian eateries, this one stands out. Starting with warm bread to dip in extra-virgin olive oil with fresh chopped garlic to large, crisp salads, to pastas and grilled meat entrées, this is a hit for diners of all ages. When Ben and Jerry (of Ben & Jerry's ice cream) take their children out, it is for a meal here. Church St. downstairs, Burlington. Open for lunch and dinner Monday-Saturday, dinner only on Sunday. $-$$. 802-660-9533.

Sneakers. This, along with Shelburne Farms, is one of the two best places for breakfast in the area. The ingredients are always fresh, and popular items include waffles, homemade granola, and eggs Benedict. Arrive early on weekends; the waiting line can wind out into the street, but it is worth the wait. 36 Main St., Winooski. Open daily for breakfast, lunch, and Sunday brunch. $. 800-448-9081 (in Vermont), 802-655-9081.

home overlooking the lake. Shore Acres and **Ruthcliffe Lodge & Restaurant** both have small, simple rooms with lake views and scenic grounds (Champlain Island Cycling rents bicycles on the premises). A good bet for bargain hunters is the **Terry Lodge of Isle La Motte,** where the rooms are plain but the food plentiful. For dinner, Shore Acres offers fresh fish, steaks, and chops; and Ruthcliffe serves American food with an Italian touch (try the garlicky shrimp Marco).

Day Three

After breakfast, plan to explore Isle La Motte. Marble and limestone from five quarries here were used in such places as the Brooklyn Bridge and the Massachusetts State House; the stone is full of fossils, evidence of the time when this region was under a predecessor of the Atlantic Ocean. Evidence of more recent history can be seen at the **1840 South School House,** a museum run by the Isle La Motte Historical Society. Nearby is **Saint Anne's Shrine,** at the site where Fort Saint Anne, Vermont's first white settlement, was built in 1666. The shrine draws thousands of Catholic pilgrims to this otherwise quiet island; one corner of the wooden open-air chapel is filled with crutches cast off by those whose prayers were answered. The Edmundite Fathers allow public use of their picnic area and sandy beach.

Then, as you head home (from Route 129, take Route 2 north to Route 78 and take the bridge into Swanton to I-89 south), you'll still have sand between your toes.

– Sheryl Lechner

Essentials

Lake Champlain Regional Chamber of Commerce, Box 453, 60 Main St., Suite 100, Burlington, VT 05401. 802-863-3489.

Champlain Islands Chamber of Commerce, P.O. Box 213, North Hero, VT 05474. 802-372-5683.

Frog Hollow on the Marketplace, 85 Church St., Burlington. Monday-Wednesday 10-6, Thursday-Saturday 10-9, Sunday noon-6. 802-863-6458.

Radisson Hotel Burlington, 60 Battery St., Burlington. Double room $109-$179. 800-333-3333, 802-658-6500.

Parima, 185 Pearl St., Burlington. Open daily for dinner 4:30-10. $-$$. 802-864-7917.

Daily Planet, 15 Center St., Burlington. Open for lunch and dinner daily. $-$$. 802-862-9647.

Al's French Frys, Williston Rd., South Burlington. Open daily 10:30 A.M.-11 P.M. 802-862-9203.

Fresh Market Cheese Outlet, 400 Pine St., Burlington. Open Monday-Saturday 8-7, Sunday 10-5. 802-863-3968.

Lake Champlain Chocolates, 431 Pine St., Burlington. Open Monday-Friday 9:30-5:30, Saturday 9:30-5, Sunday 11:30-5. 802-864-1808.

Mirabelles, 198 Main St., Burlington. Open Monday-Friday 7:30-6, Saturday 8:30-6. 802-658-3074.

Sand Bar State Park, at the causeway to the islands. Open Memorial Day through Labor Day 10-sunset. 802-893-2825.

Lake Champlain Transportation Company, Rte. 314, Grand Isle. Open year-round daily 5 A.M.-1 A.M. Ferry to Plattsburgh, N.Y., passengers $3.25 round-trip, two passengers with car $18.75. 802-372-5550.

Grand Isle Fish Culture Station, Rte. 314, Grand Isle. Open daily year-round 7:30-4. 802-372-3171.

Hyde Log Cabin, Rte. 2, Grand Isle. Open July 4-Labor Day, Wednesday-Sunday 9:30-5:30.

Knight Point State Park, North Hero. Open mid-May through mid-October 10-7. 802-372-8389.

Tudhope Sailing Center and Marina, Rte. 2, Grand Isle. 802-372-5320.

Knight Island State Park, call Vermont Dept. of Forests, Parks, and Recreation for information. 802-244-8711.

Shore Acres, Rte. 2, North Hero. Double room $77-$135, meals daily in season. $-$$$. 802-372-8722.

Island Craft Shop, Rte. 2, North Hero. Open mid-May through mid-October daily 10-5. 802-372-4161 (Hero's Welcome).

Hero's Welcome, Rte. 2, North Hero. Canoes and kayaks for rent 365 days, open in summer 6:30 A.M.-9 P.M., off-season 6:30-6:30. 802-372-4161.

Royal Lipizzan Stallions of Austria, North Hero. Call the Lake Champlain Islands Chamber of Commerce. 802-372-5683.

Thomas Mott B&B, Blue Rock Rd., Alburg. Double room with breakfast $75-$95. 800-348-0843, 802-796-3736.

Northland B&B, Rte. 2, North Hero. Double room with shared bath $60-$65. 802-372-8822.

Paradise Bay B&B, Kibbe Point Rd., South Hero. Double room with shared bath and full breakfast $75-$95. 802-372-5393.

Ruthcliffe Lodge & Restaurant, Old Quarry Rd., Isle La Motte. Double room $60-$97. $-$$$. 802-928-3200.

Terry Lodge of Isle La Motte, West Shore Rd., Isle La Motte. Double room with breakfast $65-$75, with breakfast and dinner $90-$105, some shared baths. 802-928-3264.

1840 South School House, corner Old Quarry Rd. and Rte. 129, Isle La Motte. Open July-August Saturday 2-4.

Saint Anne's Shrine, West Shore Rd., Isle La Motte. Open May-October daily 9-6. 802-928-3362.

Summer Splendor in the Northeast Kingdom

LIKE PEARY AT THE POLE, MANY VERMONT TRAVELERS reach St. Johnsbury and figure they've gotten as far north as they're going to get. But while "Saint Jay" makes a great destination, there are a lot more summertime rewards to be enjoyed in the heart of the Northeast Kingdom.

Day One

Before pressing on from St. Johnsbury, visit two premier attractions in this shire town of Caledonia County. The **Fairbanks Museum** has fascinating natural science and ethnography collections and a marvelous little planetarium. The **St. Johnsbury Athenaeum,** a perfectly preserved 1871 art gallery, houses more than a hundred Victorian landscape, portrait, and still-life paintings in a wing of the library. The star is Albert Bierstadt's breathtaking *Domes of the Yosemite,* which covers an entire wall.

Now you're ready to take off into the hinterlands of the Northeast Kingdom. Steer north on Route 5 toward Lyndonville. Then follow Route 114 north, bearing left just beyond Lyndonville onto Darling Hill Road. The big yellow and white Georgian mansion on the right was built by wealthy squire E. A. Darling, who established the model

Mountain View Farm here in 1883. The **Inn at Mountain View Creamery** was created from the Darling Farm's dairy buildings. "Mountain View" is no empty cliché: Darling Hill Road offers some of the Kingdom's most splendid panoramas. The inn has also added a restaurant with an international flair and wine list. The road ends at East Burke — a good place to start thinking about lunch.

Stop at **Bailey's Country Store,** an old ark of a place, to stock up for a picnic on a Northeast Kingdom mountaintop. Drive toward the Northern Star/Burke Mountain ski area, and take the summit road up 3,267-foot Burke Mountain. (The steep road makes many sharp turns, so be sure your brakes, radiator, and clutch are in good condition.) The observation knoll views take in a great swath of the Kingdom from the Connecticut River valley to the Green Mountains. These vistas are a great summertime treat — not even skiers get up this far.

Return to East Burke and take the back road north to West Burke and Route 5A. Driving north along 5A, you'll see the twin sentinels of Mount Hor (left) and Mount Pisgah rising abruptly above the Kingdom's crown jewel, Lake Willoughby. From its steep granite walls to the intense blue of its water, five-mile-long Willoughby resembles a landlocked fjord, suggestive of the cold 300-foot-plus depths that are the domain of record lake trout. Rent an outboard at **Bill & Billie's Lodge,** or take a dip at the little beach on the lake's warmer, shallower northern tip. By now, you might think about putting up for the night. A good choice is the **Willoughvale Inn,** with rooms, cabins, a good restaurant, and a spacious veranda that looks south into soft, mountain-framed Willoughby twilights.

Day Two

Route 5A wanders north from Lake Willoughby through wooded, sparsely populated terrain, where the cold, clear Clyde River rushes north to Lake Memphremagog via a

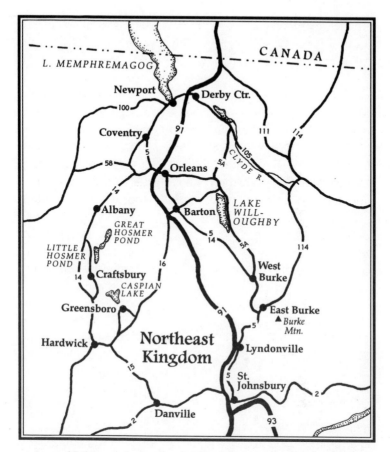

string of lakes and ponds. Continue on 5A to Derby Center; then take Route 5 into Newport, which nestles along the lake's southern American shore. Compact Newport is finally coming to terms with its incomparable lakeside location. Stroll the docks at the handsome new Gateway Center at the Waterfront to admire sleek sailing craft — many boats are down from Quebec, and there's always a touch of French in the air — or look out onto a lake that reaches north through the mountains more than 30 miles beyond the border. If the Memphremagog vistas are too tempting for you to remain shorebound, hop aboard *Newport's Princess,* a replica stern-wheeler that offers brunch, pizza, dinner, and moonlight

Surrounded by mounts Hor and Pisgah and miles of undeveloped state forest, Lake Willoughby remains one of Vermont's finest treasures. (courtesy Vermont Tourism and Marketing)

cruises. If you're staying ashore, the best bet for lunch is the **East Side Restaurant and Pub,** with a terrace overlooking the lake. Real landlubbers can turn their backs on the water altogether and explore Main Street's growing number of small discount outlet shops.

Take Route 5 south through Coventry and Orleans. On

the outskirts of Barton is **Crystal Lake State Park,** a fine place to while away a warm afternoon. The lake has a sandy, gently graded swimming beach, full bathhouse facilities, and plenty of room for picnicking, cookouts, sunbathing, and falling asleep with the newspaper. Drop south on Route 16 and take one of the back roads that meander westward through the scattered settlements and wide-horizoned meadows of Albany and Craftsbury. For a real treat, head northwest on the Bend Road from Greensboro Bend toward Caspian Lake with its 100-year-old tradition of attracting writers and educators (see "What the Locals Know"). Nowhere in Vermont is it easier to get lost than on these gorgeous byways, and nowhere will you mind it less. Just be sure you end up in Craftsbury Common, which makes everyone's list of the prettiest villages in the state. The

200 AUTHORS IN ONE TOWN

WHAT THE LOCALS KNOW

No other town the size of Greensboro can boast 200 authors. OK, some have just summered here, but no matter, the list is impressive: Supreme Court Chief Justice William Rehnquist, "Ask Beth" columnist Beth Winship, Pulitzer Prize-winner Wallace Stegner, anthropologist Margaret Mead, journalist John Gunther, and many, many others. One of the first writers to discover the sanctuary on the shores of Caspian Lake was Bliss Perry, a Princeton scholar who brought his family here in 1897. Perry later worked at Harvard, Williams, and *The Atlantic Monthly,* spreading the word to colleagues about this summer colony of writers. The locals know that the best place to go on a rainy day is the Greensboro Free Library, where the "Greensboro Authors" shelf weighs in with about 400 volumes on subjects from molecular biology to poetry, to Harlequin romances, westerns, and more. Reading and writing are such an important pastime that the library has even opened a little branch in the Greensboro Bend Store.

Greensboro Free Library, Main St., Greensboro. Open in summer Monday-Friday 10-4, Saturday 10-1; in winter Monday-Friday 10-1 and 3-5, Saturday 10-1. 802-533-2531.

common itself is a serene public park in the middle of a settlement where it might appear that everyone must be issued 50 gallons of white paint a year. For lodging, try the country elegance of the **Inn on the Common,** with its highly regarded dining room and extraordinary wine cellar. Or choose the down-home **Craftsbury B&B on Wylie Hill.**

Day Three

For an off-road perspective of Craftsbury and environs, rent a mountain bike at the **Craftsbury Outdoor Center** to ride the trail network lacing the forested hills around Hosmer Pond. The center also has a renowned sculling program — the gold-medal-winning 1996 Danish Olympic team trained here — and novices and more experienced rowers can sign up for weekend or weeklong sessions. It's a short drive south on Route 14 to Hardwick, then east via routes 15 and 2 through Danville toward St. Johnsbury. Along the way, appease that mountain-bike appetite in Danville. Stop by the **Creamery,** where Danville native Marion Beattie grinds her own beef for a terrific burger. This little town is also home of the **Danville Morgan Horse Farm,** where more than a dozen superb specimens of Vermont's state animal roam meadows overlooking New Hampshire's White Mountains. If you finish the loop early, there will be time to duck into the St. Johnsbury Athenaeum for another look at *Domes of the Yosemite,* but by now you've probably decided that the peaks and valleys of the Northeast Kingdom aren't so bad, either.

– William G. Scheller

E s s e n t i a l s

Northeast Kingdom Chamber of Commerce, 30 Western Ave., St. Johnsbury 05819. 802-748-3678.

Fairbanks Museum, Main and Prospect sts., St. Johnsbury. Open September-June Monday-Saturday 10-4; July-August Monday-Saturday 10-6, Sunday 1-5. Adults $4, seniors $3, children 5-17 $2.50, families $10. 802-748-2372.

St. Johnsbury Athenaeum, 30 Main St., St. Johnsbury. Open all year, Monday-Wednesday 10-8; Tuesday, Thursday, Friday 10-5:30, Saturday 9:30-4. 802-748-8291.

Inn at Mountain View Creamery, Darling Hill Rd., East Burke. Double room with breakfast $100-$140. Dinner in summer Thursday, Friday, Saturday. $$-$$$. 802-626-9924.

Bailey's Country Store, Rte. 114, East Burke. Open all year Monday-Saturday 7 A.M.-8 P.M., Sunday 7-7. 802-626-3666.

Bill & Billie's Lodge, Rte. 5A, Westmore. Open in summer 7-5 (no rentals after 3). 802-525-6660.

Willoughvale Inn, Rte. 5A, Westmore. Double room $99-$125. $-$$. 802-525-4123.

Newport's Princess, City Dock, Newport. Daily sailings in summer, $9.75-$24.95. 802-334-6617.

East Side Restaurant and Pub, 25 Lake St., Newport. Open for lunch and dinner daily. $-$$. 802-334-2340.

Crystal Lake State Park, Barton. Open daily seasonally. Adults $1.50, children 4-13 $1. 802-525-6205.

Inn on the Common, Craftsbury Common. Double room with breakfast and dinner $220-$280. 800-521-2233, 802-586-9619.

Craftsbury B&B on Wylie Hill, Craftsbury Common. Double room with breakfast $60-$75. 802-586-2206.

Craftsbury Outdoor Center, Craftsbury Common. Open every day in summer, $6 per hour mountain bike rental. 800-729-7751, 802-586-7767.

Creamery, Hill St., Danville. Open for lunch Tuesday-Friday. $. 802-684-3616.

Danville Morgan Horse Farm, Joe's Brook Rd., Danville. Open daily. 802-684-2251.

The Best Vermont Foliage Tour We've Ever Found

THIS 185-MILE ITINERARY COVERS A BIG CHUNK OF Vermont's northwestern corner, some of the most unvarnished and underpopulated corners of the land o' leaves. Remember, though, that foliage season is mighty popular — be sure to have your inn reservations in hand before setting out, especially if you are traveling on the weekend. Begin by taking Route 2 (Williston Road) east from Burlington, stopping for picnic supplies at **Cheese Traders.** You'll be in the country when you reach Richmond, 12 miles away. Our route calls for a left at the town's only intersection, but if you want to see the famous **Round Church,** turn right, cross the bridge, and look to the left. The church, built in 1813, actually has 16 sides.

Turn back to Richmond, head north on Jericho Road, and continue five miles to Jericho Center. The marker on the green commemorates Wilson "Snowflake" Bentley, a turn-of-the-century Jericho farmer who took the first photographs of snowflake crystals. Continue beyond Jericho Center on Brown's Trace Road for three miles to Route 15, then turn right. Ahead and a bit to the right stands Mount Mansfield — that's the chin of the mountain's illustrious profile farthest to the left (north); the nose and forehead lie farther south. (Use your imagination.)

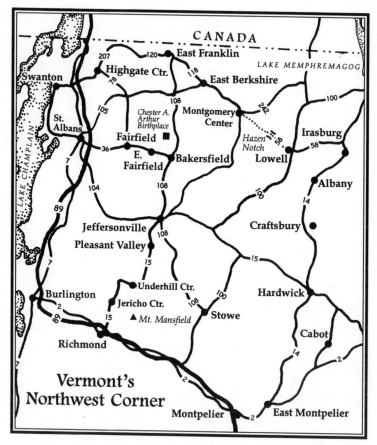

Vermont's
Northwest Corner

Stay on Route 15 for half a mile, then bear right and continue three miles to Underhill Center. Head straight through town to Pleasant Valley Road, watching for a sign a mile north for Underhill State Park, where some of the best Mount Mansfield hiking trails begin. Although there are signs, your best bet is to carry a copy of the Green Mountain Club's revised *Long Trail Guide*. A ramble along the old CCC Road or Cantilever Rock Trail offers a way to see the colors at less than highway speed.

Return to Pleasant Valley Road and follow this rolling byway north through woodlands and meadows, bearing right at the fork six miles ahead to Upper Valley Road, which delivers you to Jeffersonville by way of dairy farms and some fine views of the Lamoille River valley. For dinner take a detour south about 15 miles on Route 108 to Stowe for an abundance of dinner choices. **Edson Hill Manor** and **Ten Acres Lodge,** located in Stowe, are inns owned by Jane and Eric Lande that consistently receive rave reviews for their dining, which is open to the public. You can take a gondola ride up Mount Mansfield to the **Cliff House.** For an overnight in Austrian style, book a room at the mountaintop **Trapp Family Lodge.** Closer to Jeffersonville on Route 108 is **Smugglers' Notch Resort,** where both formal and informal dining choices abound.

Next day, head north from Jeffersonville on Route 108. At Bakersfield, the blip in the road ten miles north, turn left opposite the cemetery onto unmarked Route 36. Three miles west is East Fairfield, where you turn right, then right again three miles ahead to the reconstruction of President Arthur's family home, known as the **President Chester A. Arthur State Historic Site.** Here you will get an idea of what a wilderness this was in 1830. It still is. Stay on Route 36 through East Fairfield, and in five miles you'll enter Fairfield, where you can pick up a sandwich, a maple-walnut scone, or a whole pie at **Chester's in the Square.**

When you crest a hill six miles west of Fairfield, you may have trouble paying attention to the road. The view that suddenly spreads before you takes in a vast swath of the upper Champlain valley, with St. Albans in the foreground, Lake Champlain in the middle distance, and New York's Adirondacks as a backdrop for it all. St. Albans is a redbrick period piece; a century ago it was northern New England's rail capital. During the Civil War, it was the site of the conflict's northernmost action, when Confederate raiders robbed the town's banks and made off into Canada. Stop to appreciate the handsomely preserved Victorian facades on Main Street and the stately public buildings facing the park on Church Street. One of these houses is the **St. Albans Historical Museum,** with an eclectic trove ranging from railroadiana to an old-time doctor's office. For lunch, try **Jeff's Maine Seafood.**

Head west out of town on Route 36 (Lake Street) for three miles to St. Albans Bay. Turn right and follow Route 36 for ten miles along Lake Champlain to Swanton, gateway to the waterfowl-rich Missisquoi National Wildlife Refuge, west of town via Route 78, and a good place to stretch your legs. Continue your itinerary on Route 78 east and drive five miles to Highgate Center (intersection with Route 207). Stay on 78 east out of Highgate Center, and after about 1.5 miles,

Clear weather, no bugs, and breathtaking foliage — you'll find no better family fun than hiking Vermont in the autumn. (courtesy Vermont Tourism and Marketing)

turn left at a cluster of big gray silos onto an unmarked gravel road, which will take you through five miles of dairy country. Franklin County is Vermont's milk-producing leader; the local St. Albans Co-Op is the supplier of much of the cream that goes into Ben & Jerry's ice cream. There's a fork in this gravel road (not the four-way intersection, but the actual fork beyond it); either choice brings you to tiny Franklin, which, if everyone sneezed at once, would be in Quebec. Turn left here and bear right onto Route 120 north. Ahead and a little to the right, you'll see the summit of Jay Peak, with its cantilevered aerial tramway station. On your right, a few miles farther, Lake Carmi reflects the colors of the surrounding hills. Stay on Route 120 through East Franklin, then take Route 108 south to the junction with Route 105. Turn left and head east along the Missisquoi River to East Berkshire, where you take Route 118 south to Montgomery Center, a dining and lodging focus for the year-round resort at Jay Peak.

If you turn in for the night at the **Inn on Trout River** with its cheery Victorian rooms, you can also stay for dinner at the on-premises **Lemoine's,** which specializes in grilled meats and seafood. The **Black Lantern Inn** has ten rooms in an 1803 brick house and six suites in an adjacent house. Another dinner option is the eclectic and eccentric **Zack's on the Rocks,** where the crispy duckling and tournedos béarnaise are as much of a draw as the hanging-gardens dining room.

For the last word in foliage panoramas, take Route 242 from Montgomery Center to the **Jay Peak Tramway**. Trams run every half hour. Have an early lunch back in Montgomery Center at **J. R.'s,** where the standout sandwich is roasted eggplant with garlic mayonnaise. Some might say it's worth the drive to Vermont in itself. For an afternoon encounter with the leaves, head east from Montgomery Center through Hazen's Notch on Route 58, a gravel road through deep woods ablaze with the yellow foliage of birches. Where the Long Trail crosses the road, you find that the

Green Mountain Club's Hazen's Notch Camp is a good hiking and picnic destination 0.6 mile north of the road.

After ten miles, Route 58 crosses Route 100 (and turns to blacktop) at Lowell; continue for eight miles to Irasburg, looking north along the way for some of the best long-distance views. Just before Irasburg, you'll come to a T intersection; turn right onto Route 14, which you'll follow through town and to points south. Route 14 out of Irasburg follows the Black River, which flows north into Lake Memphremagog. As you drive south through the valley's pastures and hay fields, you'll notice left-hand turnoffs for the secondary roads through the Albanys and the Craftsburys, each town with elegant inns and restaurants that could seduce you to extend your trip. But don't let Laura Ashley fool you — this is still wild country. Near Lake Elligo, which hugs Route 14 in Craftsbury, researchers recently identified scat proving the long-debated existence of mountain lions in Vermont.

Stay on Route 14 through Hardwick, 24 miles south of Irasburg, and continue for 19 miles of lake-strewn, wooded country to East Montpelier. En route, detour to Cabot (left turn at Woodbury) for a tour of **Cabot Creamery.** At East Montpelier pick up Route 2 west for the final seven miles into Montpelier, and finish your trip with the golden dome of the state capitol rising before you. By now, you should know why it's topped with a statue of Ceres, the Roman goddess of agriculture — and why, perhaps, she should be clutching a sheaf of autumn leaves.   – *William G. Scheller*

E s s e n t i a l s

Lake Champlain Regional Chamber of Commerce, Box 453, 60 Main St., Suite 100, Burlington, VT 05401. 802-863-3489.

Stowe Area Association, Box 1320, Stowe, VT 05672. 800-247-8693, 802-253-7321.

St. Albans Chamber of Commerce, 132 North Main St., St. Albans, VT 05478. 802-524-2444.

Cheese Traders, 1186 Williston Rd., South Burlington. Open Monday-Saturday 10-7, Sunday 11-5. 802-863-0143.

Round Church, Bridge St., Richmond. Open during October daily 10-4. 802-434-2556.

Long Trail Guide, from Green Mountain Club, RR 1 Box 650, Waterbury Center, VT 05677. Members $11.95, nonmembers $14.95, plus $3.25. 802-244-7037.

Edson Hill Manor, 1500 Edson Hill Rd., Stowe. Open for dinner in season daily, off-season Friday and Saturday only, 6-10 P.M. $$$, reservations required. 802-253-7371.

Ten Acres Lodge, 14 Barrows Rd., Stowe. Open daily for dinner in season, off-season Friday and Saturday only, 6-10 P.M. $$$, reservations required. 802-253-7638.

Cliff House, Stowe Mountain Resort, Stowe. Open for dinner Thursday, Friday, Saturday. Fixed price $39. 802-253-3665.

Trapp Family Lodge, Trapp Hill Rd., Stowe. Double room with breakfast and dinner September 20 to October 13 $272. 800-826-7000, 802-253-8511.

Smugglers' Notch Resort, Rte. 108, Jeffersonville. Double room $99. 800-451-8752, 802-644-8851.

President Chester A. Arthur State Historic Site, East Fairfield. Open through October 13, Wednesday-Sunday 11-5. Admission by donation. 802-828-3051.

Chester's in the Square, Sheldon Rd., Fairfield. Open daily. 802-827-3974.

St. Albans Historical Museum, Church St., St. Albans. Open Tuesday-Saturday 1-4. 802-527-7933.

Jeff's Maine Seafood, 65 North Main St., St. Albans. Open Monday-Saturday 11:30-3. 802-524-6135.

Inn on Trout River, Rte. 118, Montgomery Center. Double room with breakfast $86. 800-338-7049, 802-326-4391.

Lemoine's at the Inn on Trout River, Rte. 118, Montgomery Center. Open for dinner nightly. $$-$$$. 800-338-7049, 802-326-4391.

Black Lantern Inn, Rte. 118, Montgomery village. Double room with breakfast $85-$145. 800-255-8661, 802-326-4507.

Zack's on the Rocks, Rte. 58, Montgomery Center. Open Tuesday-Sunday for dinner. $$$, reservations required. 802-326-4500.

Jay Peak Tramway, Rte. 242, Jay. Open Labor Day-September 15 weekends only 10-5, September 21-October 14 daily 10-5. Adults $8, seniors and juniors $5, family $25. 802-988-2611.

J. R.'s, Main St., Montgomery Center. Open for lunch daily at 11. $. 802-326-4682.

Cabot Creamery, Main St., Cabot. Open June-October 31 daily 9-5, November-May Monday-Saturday 9-4, closed in January. $1. 802-563-2231.

Day Trip: Weston, A New England Classic

WESTON, *LOCATED IN SOUTH-CENTRAL VERMONT, IS A* great jumping-off point for exploring the southern part of the state. Even if you don't have a lot of time for travel, consider Weston as a perfect destination for a day trip. This little town of 500 has the best of New England's offerings — classic architecture (lovingly preserved) dotting a maple-lined town common, history, culture (the state's oldest professional theater), and shops (the original Vermont Country Store) filled with quality goods and local handcrafts. Summer and fall are my favorite seasons here and the time when most of the local attractions are in high gear.

Few people visit Weston without stopping first at the **Vermont Country Store.** I've heard most shoppers spend an average of two hours browsing though miles of interesting and practical items, from bag balm to cotton hosiery. Vrest Orton established the store in 1946 and at the same time pioneered the mail-order industry with a catalog that today accounts for nearly 75 percent of the Ortons' multimillion-dollar business. After a couple of hours of shopping, choose the **Bryant House,** right next door, for lunch. The restaurant serves sandwiches, salads, chicken pot pie, Indian pudding, and other traditional New England fare. They don't take reservations here, but it is owned and operated by the Vermont Country Store, so they will happily take your name if the restaurant is busy, and you can head into the store for more shopping while you wait for your table.

If a picnic is more your style, pick up a sandwich at the shop in the Mill Yard and settle on the grass of the Weston Green, perch in the Weston bandstand, or find a spot on the back lawn of the Weston Playhouse. This view overlooking the West River mill falls is a local favorite.

Don't limit your shopping experience to the Vermont Country Store. In the village and on the north end of town you'll find a wide assortment of shops that sell local crafts and goods. Quilts, glass jewelry, fudge, tin works, and woodenware are just a few of the things that you'll discover are made right in Weston. At the south end of the village the **Todd Gallery** displays fine watercolors, oil paintings, prints, photography, and other works by Vermont artists.

By early afternoon the **Farrar Mansur House** will be open. Spend some time here; it is a gem, and you won't be disappointed. Built by Captain Oliver Farrar in 1797 as a tavern and inn, this house has been the setting for much of Weston's activities, from town meetings to church services, dances, and plays. The taproom and ballroom have been restored, and throughout the house antique clothing, furniture, and accessories (all from Weston families) are displayed. In the 1930s WPA artists painted outstanding murals depicting Weston as it was 100 years earlier. Behind the house, the Old Mill Museum, with its collection of wonderful antique tools, is also worth a visit.

If a day of shopping and touring has you in need of some quiet, drive north on Route 100 and turn left on Greendale Road. This road (closed in the winter) leads to the snug Greendale Campground with its 11 sites, beyond which there is a network of trails frequented by hikers and cross-country skiers. Here you'll find wooded walking paths and old logging roads in the **Green Mountain National Forest** (maps available at the district office).

No trip to Weston is complete without taking in a play at the **Weston Playhouse.** *(courtesy Weston Playhouse)*

Just a little north on Route 155, another spot for peace is the **Weston Priory,** a community of Benedictine monks formed in the 1950s when Abbot Leo Rudloff rehabilitated a run-down farm. In 1971 the brothers, whose Sunday prayer services had begun attracting hundreds of people, began recording their singing. Their music, songbooks, Guatemalan handcrafts, cards, and children's books are available at the priory's gift shop. The grounds, where you are welcome to picnic, are lovely and the stone chapel a perfect place for contemplation.

Though the day feels complete at this point, sit tight — the best is yet to come. The choice tonight is between the **Weston Playhouse** and a concert at Kinhaven. The Weston Playhouse is made up largely of professional actors, whose performances consistently receive excellent reviews. Throughout the summer there are shows most evenings and Wednesdays and Saturday afternooons. This is an exceptional theater, and no trip to Weston is complete without seeing a play. In October the Weston Playhouse hosts topnotch weekend events: an antiques show, a crafts exhibit, and on the third weekend a play. The **Kinhaven Music School** is a nationally known summer music camp that holds free concerts. Generally students perform at 2:30 on Fridays and Sundays and faculty at 8:00 on Saturday evenings. The quality of even the student concerts is extraordinary. (Call ahead to confirm this schedule.)

Now that you're sure to stay for the evening, dinner is the next decision. In the summer Weston Playhouse theatergoers often eat downstairs where the **Inn at Weston** sets up a dining room. The food is tasty, and the proximity to the theater eliminates any anxiety about getting to the show on time. You can also have a lovely dinner at the actual inn, which is known for its spacious dining rooms and fine food. If you're in the mood to treat yourself, go to the **Three Clock Inn** in South Londonderry. Chef and proprietor Serge Roche prepares American cuisine strongly influenced by his background in southern France. The food is outstanding, and for $35 each he serves a full dinner including appetizer and dessert. The wine list includes a number of labels from small French vineyards hand-selected by Serge and his wife. If you are planning to take in a play, make an early reservation here, and leave yourself about 15 minutes for the drive back to Weston.

— Polly Bannister

E s s e n t i a l s

Manchester and the Mountains Chamber of Commerce, 2 Main St., RR 2, Box 3451, Manchester Center, VT 05255. 802-362-2100.

Londonderry Area Chamber of Commerce, intersection of rtes. 11 and 100 in the Mountain Marketplace, P.O. Box 58, Londonderry, VT 05148. 802-824-8178.

Vermont Country Store, Main St. Open Monday-Saturday 9-5. 802-824-3184.

Bryant House Restaurant, Main St. Open for lunch daily 11:30-3, off-season 11:30-2. 802-824-6287.

Todd Gallery, 614 Main St. Open Thursday-Monday 10-5. Closed April. 802-864-5606.

Farrar Mansur House, on the village green. Open July and August Wednesday-Saturday, late May-late October weekends, 1:30-4:30. Adults $2, children $1. 802-824-6718.

Manchester District Office of the Green Mountain National Forest, Rte. 11/30, Box 1940, Manchester Center, VT 05255. 802-362-2307.

Weston Priory, Rte. 155. Chapel, picnic area, visitor's center, gift shop open daily 10:30-5. 802-824-5409.

Weston Playhouse, on the village green. For performance information write P.O. Box 216, Weston, VT 05161. Performances late June-Labor Day weekend. Tickets average $20, children 14 and under $10 discount. 802-824-5288.

Kinhaven Music School, Lawrence Hill Rd. Free concerts July to mid-August. 802-824-9592.

Inn at Weston, on the green. Double room with breakfast, $75-$125. 802-824-5804.

Three Clock Inn, Middletown Rd., Londonderry. Open for dinner Tuesday-Sunday. $$-$$$. Reservations appreciated. 802-824-6327.

Massachusetts

Prescription for a Perfect Weekend in Boston

BOSTONIANS HAVE ALWAYS SOUGHT PERFECTION. FIRST we focused on our souls. When that proved impossible, we turned to learning and culture. We refined our history, art, and architecture, sifting to preserve the best. It has helped to have 368 years to practice. In that time Bostonians have created a city manageable in size, beautiful to behold, and fascinating to absorb. We did it for ourselves, but we produced an important by-product — a perfect weekend destination for visitors.

If Boston were merely refined, it would quickly become just a rarefied backdrop. Luckily it's also very real. The streets are full of real people, busily pursuing their everyday activities. The traffic laws may seem obscure to outsiders — the rotary is a Massachusetts mystery understood by few — but don't take it personally. If possible, ditch your car and take public transportation; it goes virtually everywhere you might want to go and is a bargain to boot. And consider walking — the streets are safe, the distances manageable, and the natives not as brusque as they might appear.

Day One

Start the afternoon at Faneuil Hall Marketplace to explore boutiques, pushcarts of things you never knew you needed, and lots and lots of food. On Friday and Saturday boisterous

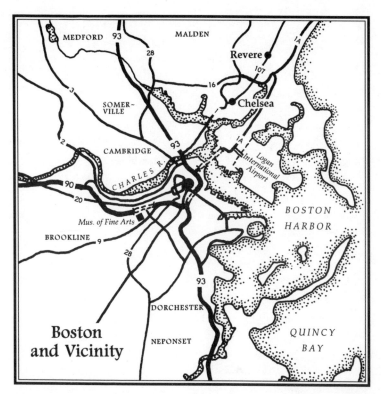

MEDFORD 93 MALDEN

Revere

28

107

3

16

SOMER-
VILLE

Chelsea

2

CAMBRIDGE 93

1A

Logan
International
Airport

CHARLES R.

90

20

Mus. of Fine Arts

BOSTON
HARBOR

BROOKLINE 9

28

93

DORCHESTER

**Boston
and Vicinity**

NEPONSET

QUINCY
BAY

Haymarket is now the outdoor produce center that Quincy Market once was. Looping around onto Union Street, look for the two bronze James Michael Curley statues honoring Boston's famous mayor and jailbird. They're right behind City Hall, widely considered the city's ugliest building. Back at the Marketplace, tour graceful Faneuil Hall (one of the nation's top attractions), where revolutionary plots were hatched. If you've wondered why grasshoppers adorn souvenir mugs, you'll find your answer on the 256-year-old weather vane perched on the hall.

Arrange ahead for tickets to the theater or take your chances at **Bostix,** Boston's cash-only, half-price, day-of-performance ticket kiosk, to choose your evening's entertainment; it's on the south side of Faneuil Hall. Before returning to your hotel, visit the Old State House. Atop this architectural jewel, the British lion and unicorn dance on the cornice.

Hotel reservations in summer need to be made well in advance. Among our favorites are the **Ritz-Carlton,** overlooking the Public Garden, elegant, proper, and oh-so-Boston; the **Omni Parker House,** on the Freedom Trail downtown; and the century-old **Copley Square Hotel,** near the Boston Public Library in Copley Square. Bed-and-breakfast devotees will find lists of agencies through the **Greater Boston Convention & Visitors' Bureau.** Complement your theater tickets with dinner at nearby Galleria Italiana. They cater to the pre-theater crowd and will get you to your show on time. For a late-night drink or snack, try the **Mercury Bar,** where the tapas get rave reviews.

Day Two

You need to travel by subway, or "T," if you are in Boston, to reach the **Museum of Fine Arts.** Take the Green Line's E trolley outbound, and get off at the Ruggles/Museum stop. Greeting you at the museum's old entrance is the *Appeal to the Great Spirit* by Cyrus Dallin, a magnificent bronze statue of a Native American on horseback, arms outstretched to the sky. To enter the museum now, you'll have to pass the statue and turn right on Museum Road. The MFA has world-renowned collections of Impressionist paintings, Egyptian artifacts, and Asian art. But what many Bostonians love most are such locally rooted treasures as are found in the Copley portrait room, where John Hancock applies his pen and Paul Revere cradles a silver teapot in his grimy fingers. Also see the Colonial silver, the European and American period rooms, and the changing special exhibits.

The **Isabella Stewart Gardner Museum,** an Italianate mansion modeled after a 16th-century Venetian palazzo, is a stunning testament to its namesake. Mrs. Gardner (or "Mrs. Jack," as she was also known) began construction of Fenway Court in 1899. Completed in 1902, it opened to the public a year later and was her residence until her death in 1924. With

If your Boston trip includes young children, don't miss the bronze duckling statues in the Public Garden. (photo by Kindra Clineff)

its spectacular inner courtyard — in bloom year-round — it houses one of the broadest collections of furniture, textiles, and art in the country, with paintings from the 13th through the 20th centuries. Both the MFA and the Gardner have inviting cafés for lunch. (At the Gardner outdoor seating is available during the summer months.)

Get back on the T inbound to the Arlington stop, and stroll up Newbury Street past galleries, trendy shops, antiques stores, and outdoor cafés in a landscape of Victorian brownstones. Cross streets are alphabetical, named after English noblemen. At Clarendon turn south to visit H. H. Richardson's Trinity Church, considered one of the great monuments of American Romanesque architecture. For a great view of the city and harbor, take the elevator to the top floor of the glass **John Hancock Tower.** Return to Newbury Street, or if you've overdosed on shopping, walk one block over to Commonwealth Avenue. Patterned after broad Parisian boulevards, this street offers a front-row view of Back Bay's elegant townhouses, the largest contiguous array of Victorian residential architecture in America. Commonwealth Avenue ends at the Public Garden, the country's first botanical garden (1837). Stroll through, taking note of the beautiful plantings and the famous swan boats.

On the far side of the Public Garden turn left onto Charles Street to reach the shopping heart of Beacon Hill. Antiques and gift stores abound; almost every doorway offers something intriguing. **Marika's** has a wonderful assortment of antique jewelry and silver; across the street, **Period Furniture Hardware** has every brass door knocker, doorknob, or doorbell you might ever need. About 10,000 people live on the 84-acre gaslit Beacon Hill. Walk up Pinckney Street, whose houses represent eras from Federal to Greek Revival. Two blocks up on your right is Louisburg Square, between Mount Vernon and Pinckney streets, long thought to be one of Boston's most fashionable addresses.

Continue up Pinckney, turn right on Joy, and turn right again on Mount Vernon. American novelist Henry James called Mount Vernon Street "the only respectable street in America." Between numbers 55 and 85 Mount Vernon are several buildings designed by Charles Bulfinch, one of America's premier architects. One block over is beautiful Chestnut Street, and Acorn Street is a picture-perfect alley that runs between Chestnut and Mount Vernon. Look for the details in the hill's brick townhouse facades: fanlights, purple windowpanes, tracery lights, boot scrapers, and unique door knockers.

For dinner Beacon Hill offers many and varied choices: **The Hungry i** is the perfect spot for an intimate dinner in a charming setting; **Lala Rokh,** on the site of the former Another Season, serves aromatic Persian-accented Middle Eastern fare such as lamb, beef, and chicken kabobs; and **Figs** brings pizza to new and dizzying heights. In the Back Bay, **Cottonwood Café** is known for its great Southwestern food and fabled margaritas.

Day Three

For Sunday brunch on Beacon Hill, try the **Hampshire**

House. The Bull & Finch Pub, better known to the universe as Cheers, is downstairs, but the atmosphere upstairs is urbane, with jazz on Sunday mornings. Then head for the Freedom Trail, the red path that leads you by some of Boston's most historic sites. Highlights include the Robert Gould Shaw Memorial, across from the State House, which commemorates the first all-black Civil War regiment in the country. The Old Granary Burying Ground is the final resting place of Paul Revere, the Boston Massacre victims, and Peter Faneuil, builder of Faneuil Hall. King's Chapel Burial Ground offers frank epitaphs and graphic depictions of death. At the Old South Meeting House, upstanding Boston citizens planned the Boston Tea Party. Incurable shoppers may veer off here down Washington Street to Filene's Basement, where Bostonians have enjoyed bargains since 1912. For lunch, bypass Faneuil Hall Marketplace for a plate of oysters at the raw bar of the 172-year-old **Union Oyster House,** or continue on the Freedom Trail under the expressway to the North End, where Bostonians as disparate as Paul Revere and Rose Fitzgerald Kennedy were born. Today this neighborhood has all the flavors and aromas of Italy; a quick lunch can be had anywhere the menu looks good, such as the acclaimed **Trattoria Il Panino.** Then it's back to history and the Freedom Trail with a visit to Paul Revere's house and Christ Church, better known as Old North Church. Finish the weekend at Copp's Hill Burying Ground on Commercial Street for a good view of Boston Harbor, which is where it all began.

– Karen Cord Taylor

E s s e n t i a l s

Greater Boston Convention and Visitors Bureau, 2 Copley Place, Suite 105, Boston 02116. Information on accommodations, sightseeing, and events 888-733-2678, 617-536-4100.

Bostix, Faneuil Hall at Quincy Market. 617-723-5181.

Ritz-Carlton, 15 Arlington St. Double room $385-$425. 800-241-3333, 617-536-5700.

Omni Parker House, 60 School St. Double room $175-$195. 800-THE-OMNI, 617-227-8600.

Copley Square Hotel, 47 Huntington Ave. Double room $175-$215. 800-225-7062, 617-536-9000.

Mercury Bar, 116 Boylston. Open nightly. 617-482-7799.

Museum of Fine Arts, 465 Huntington Ave. Open Monday, Tuesday, Thursday, and Friday 10-4:45, Wednesday 10-9:45, Saturday and Sunday 10-5:45. Adults $10, seniors and college students $8, under 17 free, Wednesday 4-9:45 P.M. by contribution. 617-267-9300.

Isabella Stewart Gardner Museum, 280 The Fenway. Open Tuesday-Sunday 11-5. Adults $9, seniors $7, college students $5, children 12-17 $3, under 12 free. 617-566-1401.

John Hancock Tower, 200 Clarendon St. Open Monday-Saturday 9 A.M.-10 P.M., Sunday 10-10. Adults $4.25, children 5-17 $3.25. 617-247-1977.

Marika's, 130 Charles St. Open Tuesday-Saturday 10-5. 617-523-4520.

Period Furniture Hardware, 123 Charles St. Open Monday-Friday 8:30-5, Saturday 10-2. 617-227-0758.

Hungry i, 71 Charles St. Open for dinner nightly 6-9, Friday and Saturday 6-10. $$$$. 617-227-3524.

Lala Rokh, 97 Mt. Vernon St. Open for dinner nightly 5:30-10. $$. 617-720-5511.

Figs, 42 Charles St. Open Monday-Friday 5:30-10, Saturday noon-10, Sunday noon-9. $-$$. 617-742-3447.

Cottonwood Café, 222 Berkeley St. Open for dinner nightly. $$-$$$. 617-247-2225.

Hampshire House, 84 Beacon St. Sunday brunch 10:30-2. $$-$$$. 617-227-9600.

Union Oyster House, 41 Union St. Open for lunch and dinner daily. $-$$$. 617-227-2750.

Trattoria Il Panino, 11 Parmenter St. Open for lunch daily. $-$$, no credit cards. 617-720-1336.

Rare June Days in Falmouth

MANY TRAVELERS THINK OF FALMOUTH, MASSACHUSETTS, only as a place to park when they catch the Vineyard ferry. In their haste they miss Falmouth village with its nigh-perfect town green, 11 harbors, and 12 miles of public beaches. We know better — and we also know that the woodlands are dotted this month with rhododendrons in full bloom, the cranberry bogs are blushing pink, and the beach roses have begun their flutter of pink and white petals.

Day One

From Boston take Route 3 toward Cape Cod. At the Sagamore Bridge traffic circle, follow Route 6 west to Buzzards Bay. Pick up Route 28 south over the Bourne Bridge. From south or west take I-495 to Route 25 to Route 28, which shoots down the west side of Cape Cod until it makes a 90-degree turn directly through Falmouth proper, the largest of the town's eight villages.

Falmouth has no shortage of superb B&Bs; aim for a central location on or near the historic town green. Good choices include the high Victorian details of the **Palmer House Inn,** the **Village Green Inn,** with its alluring front porches, and the stylish **Inn at One Main.** If you're traveling during the week, excellent bargains can be found at the somewhat motel-like rooms of **Shoreway Acres Resort Inn.**

After stopping at the chamber of commerce informa-

Nobska Lighthouse, atop a bluff in Woods Hole, commands a spectacular view of the Elizabeth Islands and the north shore of Martha's Vineyard. (photo by J. Latcham, courtesy Falmouth Chamber of Commerce)

tion center on Academy Lane for a Falmouth map, spend some time on a leisurely stroll around the village. Along the postcard-pretty town green, the white Congregational church has a bell made by Paul Revere, and the broad lawns next to St. Barnabas Church are the scene for the annual June Strawberry Festival in a town renowned for its berries. Main Street has so far escaped the Benetton franchisers, and Surf Beach is but a ten-minute walk down (what else?) Shore Street. If you're in town mid-month or later, stop by the museum of the **Falmouth Historical Society**. The main structure is a dignified Colonial built in 1790 by Dr. Francis Wicks, a medical corpsman during the Revolution and a pioneer in smallpox vaccination. The doctor's room is striking, though the amputation and bloodletting kits tell a ghoulish story.

There are many casual dinner options along Main Street, including the **Quarterdeck Restaurant.** It's a short walk to the **Coonamessett Inn,** which has a superb New American menu and a remarkable display of artwork by

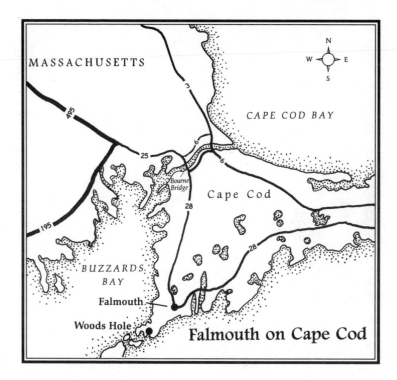

Falmouth on Cape Cod

local primitive painter Ralph Cahoon. Cahoon's paintings of mermaids and sailors in idealized 19th-century settings often sold for $200 to $300 a decade ago; last summer one canvas fetched $77,000. The free **Cahoon Museum of American Art,** in nearby Cotuit, features his work and that of other, mostly modern, "naive" painters.

Day Two

You should have the map of Falmouth from yesterday's forage at the chamber of commerce. Begin at the Old Burying Ground on Mill Road, where in 1705 Desire Bourne claimed the first grave in this Succanesset Plantation settlement. Many of the older stones are engraved with the years, months, and days of the person's life, reminding us that for these hardy settlers, every day counted. There are gravestones without graves (for sailors lost at sea) and graves without stones (for bodies washed ashore). As you continue toward the town green, you will pass a virtual history of American domestic architecture, including the home at 16 West Main Street, where Katharine Lee Bates was born. Falmouth folk may be the only ones who recall that she penned "America the Beautiful." Never mind that she moved away when she was 12; she's still celebrated as a local girl who made good. You'll be done in time to swing by **Laureen's,** a combination bake shop, café, and gourmet grocery store, for a lunch of soup and salad or the pasta of the day.

WHAT THE LOCALS KNOW

THE SWEETEST STRAWBERRIES IN NEW ENGLAND

In the 1940s East Falmouth had over 600 acres of strawberries growing. After the war, when soldiers returned with new ideas of how to make a living, farming lost its appeal, and these farms dwindled. But people on the Cape still realize that their sandy soil is perfect for certain crops — strawberries and turnips grown here are noted for their sweetness. Tony and Marina Andrews and their son, Jeffrey, and daughter-in-law Sandy run the most popular farm stand in the area, Tony Andrews's Farm Stand. They devote 12 acres to strawberries alone, and unlike some farms, the Andrewses welcome children to pick. Marina says, "We find the children are careful if we just tell them to avoid stepping on the plants." Strawberry season runs from mid-June to early July, but the Andrewses say kids and adults alike also love picking their tomatoes, green beans, and peas. In August the Andrewses hold a corn festival and invite people to pick on their 25 acres of sweet corn.

Tony Andrews's Farm Stand, 398 Meeting House Rd., East Falmouth. From the rotary in Falmouth, take Rte. 151 north, turn right on Sandwich Rd., in a mile turn left on Old Meeting House Rd., and at the fork bear right to the Andrewses' farm. Open daily June-Christmas 9-6. Strawberry picking 8-noon. 508-548-5257.

Borrow a bicycle from your B&B or walk over and rent one from **Corner Cycle.** Several bike paths share the Falmouth roads, but the Shining Sea Bike Path is a "rails-to-trails" conversion. Far from autos, it traverses a nearly flat 3.5 miles between Falmouth and the village of Woods Hole. You can stop at Trunk River Beach or pause at a marshy inlet where swans and songbirds congregate.

Woods Hole is a nautical spot with an academic bent, thanks to researchers from the Marine Biological Laboratory and the Woods Hole Oceanographic Institute. The **WHOI Exhibit Center** maintains historical exhibits and has films that are interesting. The **National Marine Fisheries Service Aquarium** has seals and lots of local fish. For a hands-on intro to marine science, call **OceanQuest** to reserve a harbor boat trip. Or stay ashore and toss back a brew and oysters at **Shuckers** before you pedal home.

Pick up your car in time to drive to Old Silver Beach (Quaker Rd., North Falmouth, off Rte. 28) for a stupendous view of the sun setting over Buzzards Bay. Dinner continues the nautical theme. The **Regatta of Falmouth-by-the-Sea** justifies its name with the view from the head of the harbor. And the imaginative menu executed with great finesse is even better than the view.

Day Three

After breakfast, pack the binoculars and drive to **Ashumet Holly and Wildlife Sanctuary.** There are 65 varieties of holly at this Massachusetts Audubon Society site, but most people come for the birds. Thirty pairs of barn swallows nesting in the barn swoop in and out in great arcs of flight. Through the year, 125 species of birds visit Ashumet; high count on a single day has been 75 species. Grab a copy of the birding checklist and head for the trails, the longest of which takes about 1½ hours.

Lunch will draw you back from the meadows and forest to the sea. Start your summer season with a real shore meal at **Green Pond Fish'n Gear.** Order some of their locally famed chowder, stuffed quahogs, and a steamed lobster. Green Pond also rents fishing gear — no license required for saltwater fishing. If you'd rather work on your slice than your cast, five golf courses in Falmouth (and one in nearby Mashpee) welcome visitors. Inquire at the chamber of commerce for a list. On your way out of town, stop by Nobska Light on Nobska Road for a last look over the beaches out to sea. (Ships can see it 17 miles away.)

— Patricia Harris and David Lyon

Essentials

Falmouth Chamber of Commerce, 1 Academy Lane, P.O. Box 582, Falmouth 02541. 800-526-8532, 508-548-8500.

Palmer House Inn, 81 Palmer Ave., Falmouth. Double room with breakfast $80-$185. 800-472-2632, 508-548-1230.

Village Green Inn, 40 Main St., Falmouth. Double room with breakfast $85-$150. 508-548-5621.

Inn at One Main, 1 Main St., Falmouth. Double room with breakfast $85-$115. 508-540-7469.

Shoreway Acres Resort Inn, Shore St., Falmouth. Double room June weekdays $45. 800-352-7100, 508-540-3000.

Falmouth Historical Society Museum, 55-65 Palmer Ave., Falmouth. Open June 15-September 15 Wednesday-Sunday 2-5. Adults $3, children 50¢. 508-548-4857.

Quarterdeck Restaurant, 164 Main St., Falmouth. Open for dinner daily 4-11. $$. 508-548-9900.

Coonamessett Inn, 311 Gifford St., Falmouth. Open for dinner daily 5-11. $$-$$$. 508-548-2300.

Cahoon Museum of American Art, 4676 Falmouth Rd., Cotuit. Open Tuesday-Saturday 10-4. 508-428-7581.

Laureen's, 170 Main St., Falmouth. Open for lunch daily 11-3. $. 508-540-9104.

Corner Cycle, 115 Palmer Ave., Falmouth. Open every day. $8/hour, $14/2-5 hours, $18/6-24 hours. 508-540-4195.

WHOI Exhibit Center, 15 Market St., Woods Hole. Open Tuesday-Saturday 10-4:30, Sunday noon-4:30. Adults $1 donation. 508-457-2000, ext. 2252 or 2663.

National Marine Fisheries Service Aquarium, corner Albatross and Water sts., Woods Hole. Open mid-June to Labor Day daily 10-4, Labor Day to mid-June Monday-Friday 10-4. 508-548-5123.

OceanQuest, Woods Hole Dock. Monday-Friday 10 A.M., noon, 2, 4 P.M.; Saturday and Sunday by reservation. Adults $15, under 12 $10, under 3 free. 800-37-OCEAN, 508-457-0508.

Shuckers, 91A Water St., Woods Hole. Open every evening. $-$$. 508-540-3850.

Regatta of Falmouth-by-the-Sea, Scranton Ave., Falmouth. Open nightly for dinner 5-10. $$$$, reservations suggested. 508-548-5400.

Ashumet Holly and Wildlife Sanctuary, 286 Ashumet Rd., East Falmouth. Open daily sunrise-sunset. Adults $3, seniors and under 17 $2. 508-563-6390.

Green Pond Fish'n Gear, 348 East Falmouth Hwy., East Falmouth. Open every day until 7 P.M. $$-$$$. 508-548-2573.

Plymouth to Provincetown in Three Days

NO MATTER HOW CLEVERLY YOU SCHEME, IF YOU VISIT the Cape in summer, you'll never elude the crowds, so you may as well count yourself among them while satisfying your own particular agenda. If you can travel midweek and stay off Route 28, the overly developed southerly route, the roads should be a relative breeze. Weekenders will want to avoid trying to cross either the Bourne or the Sagamore bridges Friday or Sunday after 3:00 or 4:00 P.M. If you find you have no choice, be prepared to crawl. In fact, you'll probably make just as good time if you take time out for supper. Some inns may require a two-day (or more) minimum stay. Reservations, of course, are a must, not just for lodging but for anything other than the most casual dining. Then again, while you may not be able to reserve a stretch of deserted beach this time of year or get a table at the top restaurants, the ubiquitous clam shacks are a democratic delight. (If you are taking this tour off-season, we recommend you call ahead for times.)

Day One
A stopover in Plymouth is not only enjoyable in its own right, but it will also help you appreciate the vestiges of

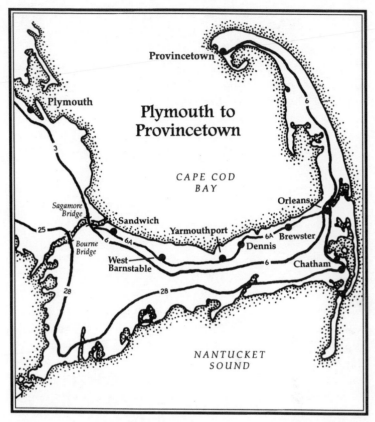

Plymouth to
Provincetown

CAPE COD
BAY

NANTUCKET
SOUND

Colonial life still visible along the Cape. Duck into the
Pilgrim Hall Museum, the nation's oldest museum.
Housed in a handsome 1824 Greek Revival building
designed by Alexander Parris (whose next project would be
Boston's Quincy Market), this vault may be dim and fusty,
but it has the goods: John Alden's halberd, William
Brewster's chair, and all sorts of odd relics. To see how well
the descendants did, pop into the **Mayflower Society
House.** For a concrete notion of the journey the Pilgrims
endured, board the replica *Mayflower II* in Plymouth
Harbor; then head a few miles south to **Plimoth Plantation,**
which re-creates the settlement circa 1627. In both venues,
highly skilled actors portray actual colonists; it's easy to get

drawn into this convincing pretend world. Give yourself a couple of hours, and finish with a look at the exhibits and lunch at the Plantation's Visitors Center.

The afternoon is young, so you have time to scoot over the Sagamore Bridge into Sandwich without enduring too lengthy a wait. Serious collectors will want to case **H. Richard Strand Antiques** en route to **Heritage Plantation,** where the collections of Josiah K. Lilly and friends deserve several hours of instructive envy. Among the must-sees: a replica Shaker round barn housing antique automobiles; an art museum strong on folk art, with a splendid 1912 carousel; and a jitney that rambles through 76 acres of dazzling rhododendrons, whose blossoms peak in May and June.

Sandwich boasts enough charming B&Bs to support a week's worth of musical beds but, alas, lacks comparable small-scale restaurants. The resurrected **Daniel Webster Inn** serves superb New American fare, if it is a bit big and bustling. It is east on historic Route 6A, a one-time native footpath known for several centuries now as the Old King's Highway, that you'll find a rich vein of restaurants. Depending on how much time you spent in the museums, you might also fit in a visit to a handful of shops in West Barnstable (all close by five o'clock): **Black's Weaving Shop, Salt & Chestnut Weather Vanes,** and **Prince Jenkins Antiques,** a downright weird but potentially rewarding trove.

Along the next ten miles are concentrated some of the most colorful eateries and sleeperies anywhere on the Cape. Tiny Yarmouthport has two inviting bistros: **Abbicci,** for accomplished nuovo Italian; and **Inaho,** a Japanese oasis. In Dennis, the **Red Pheasant Inn** occupies an 18th-century ship's chandlery and dishes up brilliant regional cuisine. Period lodgings are offered at Brewster's delightful **Bramble Inn.** For inventive fish, consider the **Brewster Fish House.** For a gastronomic blowout on a grand scale, nothing quite compares with Brewster's **Chillingsworth,** where seven classical French courses are afforded all the pomp of an affair of state. Chillingsworth now also offers a lower-priced bistro menu, served à la carte nightly in the Greenhouse. If you anticipate ending up too sated to stir, this 1689 Colonial also contains three elegant bedrooms.

Other notable hostelries along this stretch include the **Charles Hinckley House,** a shipwright-built 1809 Federal with private baths and fireplaces, awash in wildflowers; **Ashley Manor,** a cozy 1699 Colonial with tennis court; and the **Wedgwood Inn,** a formal 1812 Federal with a newly renovated carriage barn. Overlooking a weathered windmill, the **Brewster Farmhouse Inn** is severe Greek Revival on the outside, sumptuous southern California within. At the **Captain Freeman Inn,** three suites have their own Jacuzzis on private sunporches. An appealing budget option is the homey **Isaiah Hall B&B.** It's popular among the accomplished actors who perform at the nearby **Cape Playhouse,** America's oldest continuously operated summer theater, where unknowns such as Bette Davis — then an ambitious usherette — performed. Next door, disguised as a church, is the 1930 art deco **Cape Cinema,** with its dazzling Rockwell Kent mural and antimacassared leather armchairs. Rest and dream.

Day Two
Today's plan is to sneak down to Chatham, traffic be damned, and eventually press on to Provincetown. A little

---

BEST BIKING

Anyone who bikes on the Cape has heard of the Cape Cod Rail Trail, but what many folks don't know is that most kids prefer biking at Nickerson State Park. Here you'll find eight winding miles of bike trails with really steep hills that are more exciting than the smooth and gentle ride on the Rail Trail. Ask any Cape kid.

Nickerson State Park, 3488 Rte. 6A, Brewster. Open daily year-round. 508-896-3491.

west of the old-timey **Brewster General Store,** Route 137 south will lead you to the Old Queen Anne Road turnoff for Chatham, the most shoppable enclave on the Cape. As you proceed toward the sea, look for the **Munson Gallery** for contemporary art; the **Spyglass,** with optical and nautical antiques; **Chatham Cookware** for comestibles as well as utensils; **Chatham Candy Manor** for hand-dipped chocolates; **Midsummer Nights** for gourmet lingerie and hedonistic home accessories; and **Mildred Georges Antiques,** an inviting hodgepodge strong on vintage jewelry.

When you've run out of land, you'll have reached the 1828 Chatham Light, where South Beach has reattached itself to town, providing a handy place to take a dip. There are plenty of well-marked access points to the 30-mile Cape Cod National Seashore, from Nauset Beach in Orleans all the way to Provincetown's Race Point. Either arrive by 9:00, when the parking lots fill, or show up in midafternoon, when the ruddy multitudes head home.

Beach-bound or merely cruising, you can grab a feast to go at Chatham Cookware or sit down to a leisurely lunch at **Christian's,** a clubby bar with flower-bedecked patio. Head for Wellfleet as the evening approaches, for gallery hopping

Provincetown owes its natural beauty to the sea that surrounds it.
(courtesy Addison Associates)

(there are dozens; most hold their wine-and-cheese openings on Saturday night) and a light supper. The **Bayside Lobster Hutt** can provide the classic picnic-table encounter with a fresh-hauled arthropod. For those who prefer a bit more finesse, **Aesop's Tables** serves consistently enchanting regional cuisine.

For the energetic, Provincetown's nightlife awaits. P-town stores and galleries typically stay open until 10:00, which is when the colorful populace is just getting warmed up. (Day-trippers who come to gawk while the sun's still up miss the show entirely.) Park in the far east end: If you can manage it, the **Watermark Inn** is a lovely place to stay, with contemporary suites right on the water. As you head toward the epicenter, check out the galleries and the nonprofit **Provincetown Art Association and Museum.** For an aperitif with a splash of local color, stop at the sophisticated **Café Mews.** Venture inside the 1878 town hall, if it's open, to glimpse *Fish Cleaners,* an evocative portrait by Charles Hawthorne, who turned what was a drab, isolated port town into an arts mecca at the turn of the century. Even amid today's tourist hordes, you'll have ample opportunity, wandering through town, to savor the haven of creativity and tolerance he and his pioneering successors ultimately wrought.

Day Three

If morning finds you still in Provincetown, your options are many: Take a dawn-lit walk on the beach, recover over brunch, then vault up the **Pilgrim Monument.** If you've made your way back to historic Route 6A, just meander pleasurably along it, looking in on any curious shops you may have missed on your first go-through. Three days is clearly not enough time to experience all the pleasures of the Cape, but it is good for a taste, and provided you get off by early afternoon on Sunday — if you like to travel at more than three miles an hour — you'll be that much closer to coming back.

— Sandy MacDonald

Essentials

Cape Cod Chamber of Commerce, junction rtes. 6 and 132, P.O. Box 790, Hyannis, MA 02601. 888-332-2732, 508-362-3225.

Massachusetts Tourism Information Center, exit 5 on Rte. 3 (look for the big Indian carving), P.O. Box 1140, Plymouth, MA 12360. 508-746-1150.

Provincetown Chamber of Commerce, 307 Commercial St., P.O. Box 1017, Provincetown, MA 02657. 508-487-3424.

Pilgrim Hall Museum, 75 Court St., Plymouth. Open daily 9:30-4:30. Adults $5, seniors $4.50, children under 16 $3, families $13. 508-746-1620.

Mayflower Society House, 4 Winslow St., Plymouth. Open July to mid-September daily 10-4, spring and fall Friday, Saturday, and Sunday 10-4. Adults $2.50, children 6-12 25¢. 508-746-2590.

Mayflower II and Plimoth Plantation, Rte. 3, Plymouth. Open April 1-November 30 daily 9-5. Admission to both, adults $18.50, children $11. 508-746-1622.

H. Richard Strand Antiques, 2 Grove St., Sandwich. Open daily 9-5. 508-888-3230.

Heritage Plantation, Grove and Pine sts., Sandwich. Open mid-May to late October daily 10-5. Adults $9, seniors $8, children 6-18 $4.50, under 6 free (no entrance after 4:15). 508-888-3300.

Daniel Webster Inn, 149 Main St., Sandwich. Open for lunch and dinner daily. $$-$$$. 508-888-3623.

Black's Weaving Shop, 597 Rte. 6A, West Barnstable. Open daily. 508-362-3955.

Salt & Chestnut Weather Vanes, 651 Maple St., West Barnstable. Open daily. 508-362-6085.

Prince Jenkins Antiques, 975 Rte. 6A, West Barnstable. Open daily. No phone.

Abbicci, 43 Main St., Yarmouthport. Open for dinner nightly at 5. $$$. 508-362-3501.

Inaho, 157 Rte. 6A, Yarmouthport. Open for dinner nightly at 5. $$-$$$. 508-362-5522.

Red Pheasant Inn, 905 Rte. 6A, Dennis. Open for dinner nightly at 5. $$$. 508-385-2133.

Bramble Inn, 2019 Rte. 6A, Brewster. Double room $95-$125. Dinner fixed price $$$$. 508-896-7644.

Brewster Fish House, 2208 Rte. 6A, Brewster. Open for dinner nightly at 5. $$-$$$. 508-896-7867.

Chillingsworth, 2449 Rte. 6A, Brewster. Double room $95-$135. Open for dinner nightly. $$$$. 508-896-3640.

Charles Hinckley House, 8 Scudder Ln., Barnstable. Double room with breakfast $119-$149. 508-362-9924.

Ashley Manor, 3660 Rte. 6A, Barnstable. Double room with breakfast $120-$180. 508-362-8044.

Wedgwood Inn, 83 Main St., Rte. 6A, Yarmouthport. Double room with breakfast $125-$185. 508-362-5157.

Brewster Farmhouse Inn, 716 Main St., Rte. 6A, Brewster. Double room with breakfast $110-$175. 508-896-3910.

Captain Freeman Inn, 15 Breakwater Rd., Brewster. Double room with breakfast $125-$245. 508-896-7481.

Isaiah Hall B&B, 152 Whig St., Dennis. Double room with breakfast $89-$122. 800-736-0160, 508-385-9928.

Cape Playhouse, Rte. 6A, Dennis. Open seasonally. 508-385-3911.

Cape Cinema, Rte. 6A, Dennis. Open seasonally. 508-385-2503.

Brewster General Store, 1935 Main St., Rte. 6A, Brewster. Open daily 6-6. 508-896-3744.

Munson Gallery, 880 Main St., Chatham. Open daily. 508-945-2888.

Spyglass, 618 Main St., Chatham. Open daily. 508-945-9686.

Chatham Cookware, 524 Main St., Chatham. Open daily. 508-945-1550.

Chatham Candy Manor, 484 Main St., Chatham. Open daily. 508-945-0825.

Midsummer Nights, 471 Main St., Chatham. Open daily. 508-945-5562.

Mildred Georges Antiques, 447 Main St., Chatham. Open daily. 508-945-1939.

Christian's, 443 Main St., Chatham. Open daily for lunch. $$. 508-945-3362.

Bayside Lobster Hutt, 91 Commercial St., Wellfleet. Open for dinner nightly. $$-$$$. 508-349-6333.

Aesop's Tables, 316 Main St., Wellfleet. Open for dinner nightly. $$$$. 508-349-6450.

Watermark Inn, 603 Commercial St., Provincetown. Double room July $125-$265, August $135-$290. 508-487-0165.

Provincetown Art Association and Museum, 460 Commercial St., Provincetown. Open Memorial Day-Labor Day daily noon-5 and 8-10 P.M. Call for off-season hours. Adults $3, seniors and children under 12 $1. 508-487-1750.

Café Mews, 429 Commercial St., Provincetown. Open nightly. 508-487-1500.

Pilgrim Monument, High Pole Hill Rd., Provincetown. Open July-August daily 9-7; April, May, June, September, October, and November 9-5. Adults $5, children 4-12 $3, 3 and under free, last admission 45 minutes before closing. 508-487-1310.

Preseason Pleasures of the Southern Berkshires

MOST VISITORS COME TO THE BERKSHIRES FOR THE SUMMER arts and Tanglewood, though it is a bit early for these attractions. A preseason visit means there's all the more time for wandering back roads, taking a leisurely hike, poking around antiques shops, and lolling over a second glass of wine with dinner. You can catch up with Mozart later in the season.

Day One

Plan to arrive in the evening so you'll have two days to explore this region, 140 miles from both Boston and New York. From Boston take the Massachusetts Turnpike to exit 2 and Route 20 west in Lee. From New York take the Taconic State Parkway north to Route 23 east and Route 7 north. Accommodations run from rustic B&Bs to full-service resorts on historic estates. Rooms can be pricey, but May is still considered off-season. We've selected restaurants and lodgings that skip the snootiness of the high-priced spreads.

The rambling 14-room **Garden Gables Inn,** built as a private estate in 1780, fits a traveler's image of an old-fashioned country inn, with a pretty decor and a distinct shortage of right angles. There's a swimming pool and five acres of lawn and gardens. Ask for a room with a balcony.

The historic **Merrell Tavern Inn B&B** is a former stage-coach tavern built in 1794. The three-story brick inn has nine rooms, three with fireplaces, most furnished with canopy beds and 18th- and 19th-century antiques. For dinner try **La Bruschetta Ristorante.** The menu is traditional and contemporary Italian, with dishes that marry some unusual flavors — a grilled pork chop with green olive sauce or wild mushroom and spinach cannelloni.

Day Two

Drive south on Route 7 to Great Barrington for a vibrant downtown and an eclectic mix of shops. Railroad Street is worth a stroll for sublime pastries at **Daily Bread** and contemporary women's clothing at **Drygoods.** Continue on Route 7 south to Route 23 to South Egremont, a postcard New England town, where it seems to be a bylaw to keep your house painted white. Several antiques shops line this one-mile stretch, including **Splendid Peasant, Ltd.,** specializing in country furniture and folk art. As you head back toward Great Barrington, you'll see the sign for the road to Sheffield on your right. (There's no official name for this road, but the locals call it Old Sheffield Road.) It's a vintage back-country road that winds through open fields and working farms. After seven miles or so the road meets Route 7 again. Turn right and you're in antiques heaven: Some two dozen stores line Route 7, which soon becomes Sheffield's Main Street. Among the specialties are wicker at **Corner House Antiques** and American clocks and Wedgwood at **Centuryhurst Antiques.**

Maybe the best old treasures, though, are the Berkshire landscapes. More than 100,000 acres in Berkshire

County are protected from development by the state or by nonprofit groups. One of the most unusual spots is **Bartholomew's Cobble,** a rare rocky outcropping that rises 100 feet from a rolling pasture near the Connecticut border. Follow Route 7 south to Route 7A to Ranapo Road to Weatogue Road in Ashley Falls to reach this National Natural Landmark. Before you call it a day, stop for dinner at **La Tomate**, for dishes of southern France (lobster bouillabaisse, filet au poivre, and several pastas) in a lively, informal bistro setting.

Day Three
Put on your Nikes, for you'll be on the run today. First stop is the **Berkshire Botanical Gardens,** just west of Stockbridge

Center. May is a high point for the gardens, when hundreds of daffodils and the flowering cherry trees bloom. In early May look for the annual plant sale and herb fair. Toward Memorial Day the lilacs, peonies, and early specimens of mountain laurel begin to bloom. The rose garden becomes spectacular in June. Be sure to check out the woodland wildflowers whenever you go. Less than a mile south on Route 183 is the area's leading new tourist attraction, the **Norman Rockwell Museum.** The museum celebrates the life of the illustrator who single-handedly created mythological small-town America. Just down the road is **Chesterwood,** the Norman-style home of sculptor Daniel Chester French, best known for the seated Lincoln in the Lincoln Memorial. The

---

WHERE TO FIND GREAT VIEWS

WHAT THE LOCALS KNOW

Folks in Stockbridge know where in town to find a bit of wilderness — they head up behind the Stockbridge Plain School to a path that leads to **Laurel Hill.** In a grove here overlooking mountain vistas there is a rostrum, tablet, and memorial seat designed by Daniel Chester French. This is the site of the annual summer meeting of the Laurel Hill Association; founded in 1853 and taking its name from this spot, it is the oldest existing village improvement society in the United States. One of the first uses of this natural meeting place was to commemorate the death of Lafayette in 1834. The laurel-covered hill was given to the town by Theodore Sedgwick, and it remains in his words, "a presence of wild nature at the edge of the village."

Olivia's Overlook is another local favorite for a superb view of the Stockbridge Bowl. From the main entrance to Tanglewood at Route 183, drive south 0.1 mile to Richmond Road on the right. About 1.5 miles up the hill here is a panoramic view of the surrounding hills. The scenic overlook was developed by the Tennessee Gas Line Co., whose pipeline crosses the high point of Lenox Mountain. The land was donated by the Olivia Stokes Hatch family in honor of Olivia (1908-1983), an environmentalist who took great pleasure in this view across the Berkshires.

gardens and woodsy trails here are particularly lovely — daffodils and lilies of the valley bloom in May. For lunch try **Theresa's Stockbridge Café,** on the site of the original Alice's Restaurant, or try the **Lion's Den at the Red Lion Inn** for a good tavern menu. Then grab a rocking chair and hang out for a spell on the front porch.

To do the wild thing, head north on Route 7 to 7A in Lenox for the **Pleasant Valley Wildlife Sanctuary**. Follow Route 7A to West Dugway Road, across from Quality Inn, to West Mountain Road, Lenox. Several different trails meander through hundreds of acres of meadows, wetlands, and forests. There's a rustic trailside museum, and interpretive signs provide information about the landscape and its flora and fauna. And while the birding is fine (80 species breed here and the wood warblers are migrating through in May), most people come for the beavers. To see these reclusive rodents, wait quietly near the dammed beaver ponds at sunset.

If you're in town Memorial Day weekend or later and prefer nature in a more decorous mood, spend the afternoon on the grounds of **Naumkeag.** The 26-room shingled cottage was designed by Stanford White and built in 1886 for Joseph Choate, former ambassador to England. Choate's daughter Mabel was a gardening aficionada with lots of money, and the gardens designed by Fletcher Steele are the Berkshires' finest.

– B. J. Roche

E s s e n t i a l s

Berkshire Visitors Bureau, Berkshire Common, Plaza Level, Pittsfield, MA 01201. 800-237-5747, 413-443-9186.

Garden Gables Inn, 141 Main St., Rte. 7A, Lenox. Double room with breakfast $95-$205 through June, $110-$225 after July 1. 413-637-0193.

Merrell Tavern Inn Bed & Breakfast, 1565 Pleasant St., Rte. 102, South Lee. Double room with breakfast $75-$115 through June, $95-$165 July 1 through foliage season, no smoking. 800-243-1794, 413-243-1794.

La Bruschetta Ristorante, 1 Harris St., West Stockbridge. Open daily for dinner. $$$. 413-232-7141.

Daily Bread, Railroad St., Great Barrington. Open Monday-Saturday. 413-528-9610.

Drygoods, Railroad St., Great Barrington. Monday-Saturday 10-5:30, Sunday noon-5. 413-528-2950.

Splendid Peasant, Ltd., Rte. 7, South Egremont. Open daily 9:30-5:30. 413-528-5755.

Corner House Antiques, Main St., Sheffield. Open "most days" 10-5. 413-229-6627.

Centuryhurst Antiques, Main St., Sheffield. Open daily 9-5. 413-229-3277.

Bartholomew's Cobble, Weatogue Rd., Ashley. Open April 15-October 15 daily 9-5. Adults $3, children 6-12 $1. 413-229-8600.

La Tomate, 405 Stockbridge Rd., Great Barrington. Open for dinner Tuesday-Sunday. $$-$$$. 413-528-8020.

Berkshire Botanical Gardens, intersection of rtes. 102 and 183, Stockbridge. Open May 1 to mid-October daily 10-5. Adults $5, seniors $4, children 6-12 $3, under 6 free. 413-298-3926.

Norman Rockwell Museum, Rte. 183, Stockbridge. Open daily 10-5. Adults $9, children under 18 $2, families $20. 413-298-4100.

Chesterwood, Rte. 183, Stockbridge. Open May 1-October 31 daily 10-5. Adults $7.50, children 13-18 $3.50, children 6-12 $1.50, grounds ticket only $5. 413-298-3579.

Theresa's Stockbridge Café, 40 Main St., Stockbridge. Open daily. $. 413-298-5465.

Lion's Den at the Red Lion Inn, Main St., Stockbridge. Open daily June-late September noon-11. Closed midweek in off-season. $-$$. 413-298-5545.

Pleasant Valley Wildlife Sanctuary, West Mountain Rd., Lenox. Open daily dawn-dusk. Adults $3, seniors and children $2. 413-637-0320.

Naumkeag, Prospect Hill Rd., Stockbridge. Open Memorial Day-Columbus Day daily 10-5. Last tour at 4:15. Adults $7, children 6-12 $2.50. 413-298-3239.

Day Trip: Northampton, a Lot Like Cambridge — Only Better

DO YOU LIKE BOOKS? DO YOU LIKE COFFEE? DO YOU like books and coffee together? Does your taste in crafts lean toward offbeat or refined? Do your clothes say salvage or chic? And most important, do you love to shop and eat in the reassuring glow of an American bastion of learning? Well, Cambridge will do — but for great books, coffee, crafts, clothes, food, plus some fresh air and a pleasant ride — try Northampton.

From east or west take exit 4 off the Massachusetts Turnpike in West Springfield to I-91 north, then take exit 18 to Route 5 north; from north or south take exit 18 off I-91 to Route 5 north. As you enter town on Route 5 (King Street), it becomes Pleasant Street where it crosses Main. If you arrive early enough to want breakfast, continue to number 111 Pleasant where you will find **Sylvester's.** Have a leisurely breakfast, but I suggest only one coffee — many other cups await.

Turn your car around and head back up Pleasant to the lights at Main Street. Take a left, and you'll be in the heart of downtown Northampton. There's plenty of metered parking and several municipal lots, and while I wouldn't say that finding a space is always a snap, it's a dream compared to Harvard Square. The west side of Main Street (from State Street to Center Street) will entertain you for as long as you please. If you're looking for a CD or tape, stop in **B-Side Records;** it features all kinds of music. Next, if your supply of camouflage clothes needs updating, check out the **Army Barracks,** at the corner of Masonic Street. As you pass the **Fresh Pasta Company,** surely you won't be hungry yet, but peruse the menu in the window anyway as a possible lunch spot.

At number 247 you'll find the **Broadside Bookshop,** with its good selection of titles in fiction, nonfiction, history, psychology, and women's issues. Now you are entering the Coffee Zone: first up, **JavaNet** — dark, cozy, elegant, with jazz playing subtly in the background; then there's **Bart's,** for serious coffee with a bricks-and-books look (they also have homemade Kahlúa Sombrero and Black Russian ice cream for some additional caffeine-loading). Next you'll pass Starbuck's, but you've probably been there and done that, so keep going. At 189 is **Beyond Words Bookstore and Café,** with a wide offering of New Age and spiritual books. For a truly cross-cultural experience, it had a dreidel piñata in its window the day I visited. You have now arrived at the **Haymarket Café;** upstairs are two tiny tables and faux stone walls, with a funky assortment of European-looking art on the walls. Downstairs, you can curl up in an inviting nook suffused with soft light and surrounded by bookshelves. Have a latte and read some short stories.

Galleries abound along this stretch of Main Street. The **Wm. Baczek Gallery** at number 229 displays works by talented New England painters working in "contemporary American realism." For outstanding contemporary crafts and beautiful handmade clothing — wearable art, they call it — be sure to visit **Skera. Joia** has all the wonderful soaps, oils, lotions, and creams that your body could wish for. **Pinch Pottery,** at 179, is widely known for its fine ceramics. The **Mountain Goat** reminds you that you're surrounded by the great outdoors in this part of western Massachusetts, with its wool and fleece clothing and excellent stock of hiking boots.

By now you've walked but a few hundred yards, yet you've experienced a rather sophisticated array of shops for such a bucolic setting. If it's lunch you crave, return to the Fresh Pasta Company for foccacia pizza with grilled eggplant or panini with portobello mushrooms, Brie, and leeks. Or cross Main Street and wander through **Thornes Marketplace** for a happy mélange of shops. Be sure to check out Taylor Women (first floor) and Taylor Men (second floor), Strada Shoes, and the Cedar Chest — stylish enough for any Cantabrigian.

Don't miss a chance to visit the **Words and Pictures Museum,** just down the block from Thornes Marketplace. It's a one-of-a-kind experience that features interactive contemporary art, especially the original art drawn for comic books. They have four galleries, and upstairs is the Interactive Zone, with touch-screen computers and drawing tables. (Hold on to your crayons, kids; adults love it.)

You might want to retrieve your car now. Even if you've neglected to feed the meter, a parking ticket is a mere $5. Head up upper Main Street toward Smith College (the aforementioned bastion). Park on Green Street and find your way across campus to the **Lyman Plant House and Smith College Botanic Gardens.** This sprawling 19th-century conservatory will instantly transport you to a lush jungle, a temperate flowering paradise, or a desert landscape, depending on which greenhouse you happen into. It's a balm to all your senses. Then wander around the Smith campus and remark at all the architectural uses brick has been put to in the last 122 or so years.

Stroll down Green Street if you possibly need any more books, coffee, or jewelry, to end at the **Green Street Café** for a fabulous dinner. Consider New Zealand cockles with capellini, lamb shank braised in red wine, or fireplace-roasted duck with figs. Sip your coffee (yes, more coffee), and contemplate a leisurely drive back home. Or if you get a second wind, call the **Iron Horse Music Hall** or the **Academy of Music Opera House** to see what's scheduled for that night. What a fine day you've had — all the citified pleasures, few of the citified annoyances, and all the countrified charm.

– Louise Clayton

Essentials

Sylvester's, 111 Pleasant St. Open for breakfast daily at 7. 413-586-5343.

B-Side Records, 273 Main St. Open Monday and Tuesday 9:30-6, Wednesday 9:30-8, Thursday-Saturday 9:30-9, Sunday noon-6. 413-586-9556.

Army Barracks, 257 Main St. Open Monday-Wednesday 10-7, Thursday-Saturday 10-9, Sunday noon-7. 413-585-9330.

Fresh Pasta Company, 249 Main St. Open Monday-Thursday 11-9, Friday and Saturday 11-10, Sunday 2-9. $. 413-586-5875.

Broadside Bookshop, 247 Main St. Open Monday-Wednesday 9:30-6, Thursday-Saturday 9:30-9, Sunday noon-6. 413-586-4235.

JavaNet, 241 Main St. Open Monday-Friday 7 A.M.-midnight, Saturday and Sunday 8 A.M.-midnight. $. 413-587-3400.

Bart's, 235 Main St. Open Monday-Thursday 7:30 A.M.-11 P.M., Friday and Saturday 7:30 A.M.-midnight, Sunday 8 A.M.-11 P.M. $. 413-584-0721.

Beyond Words Bookstore and Café, 189 Main St. Open Monday-Saturday 9:30 A.M.-10 P.M., Sunday 11-6. 413-586-6304.

Haymarket Café, 185 Main St. Open Monday-Friday 7 A.M.-midnight, Saturday and Sunday 8 A.M.-midnight. $. 413-586-9969.

Wm. Baczek Gallery, 229 Main St. Open Tuesday-Saturday 10-6, Thursday 10-8:30, Sunday 12:30-5. 413-585-2760.

Skera, 221 Main St. Open Monday-Saturday 10-5:30, Sunday 10-9. 413-586-4563.

Joia, 201 Main St. Open Monday-Wednesday and Saturday 10-6, Thursday and Friday 10-9, Sunday noon-5. 413-586-7555.

Pinch Pottery, 179 Main St. Open Monday-Saturday 10-6, Thursday 10-9, Sunday noon-5. 413-586-4509.

Mountain Goat, 177 Main St. Open Monday-Wednesday 10-6, Thursday-Saturday 10-9, Sunday noon-6. 413-586-0803.

Thornes Marketplace, 150 Main St. Open Monday-Wednesday 10-6, Thursday, Friday, and Saturday 10-9, Sunday noon-6. 413-584-5582.

Words and Pictures Museum, 140 Main St. Open Tuesday-Thursday noon-5, Friday noon-8, Saturday 10-8, Sunday noon-5. Adults $3, seniors and students $2, children $1. 413-586-8545.

Lyman Plant House and Smith College Botanic Gardens, College Lane off Elm St. Open daily 8:30-4:15. 413-585-2748.

Green Street Café, 62 Green St. Open for dinner nightly at 5:30. $$$-$$$$. 413-586-5650.

Iron Horse Music Hall, 20 Center St. Cover varies. Call for current and upcoming performances. 413-586-8686.

Academy of Music Opera House, 274 Main St. Call for show times. 413-584-8435.

Connecticut

Three Picture-
Perfect Days on
Connecticut's
Art Trail

A CENTURY AGO AMERICAN ARTISTS, JUST BACK FROM Europe with radical ideas about light and open-air painting, began riding the train from New York to the Connecticut woodlands and coast, where the play of light and the lay of the land created especially pleasing effects. As warm weather unfolds, you can bring your own fresh eyes to some of the landscapes that spawned the American Impressionist movement.

Day One
Arrive early afternoon in Greenwich, taking exit 4 from I-95. From New York turn left or from New Haven turn right at the end of the exit, and continue three-quarters of a mile to Putnam Avenue. Turn left and drive one mile to Maple Avenue, where you'll make a very sharp right. Check in at the **Stanton House Inn.** In 1900 architect Stanford White — a good friend of many American Impressionist painters — oversaw the enlargement of the Stanton House. The

24 guest rooms (22 with private baths) have unusual but cozy layouts, while the public areas embody a classic formality.

A must-see for the afternoon is the **Bush-Holley Historic House,** site of the first Connecticut art colony. This 1732 saltbox became an inn in 1884, and in 1892 artists began boarding here, led by John Twachtman, Childe Hassam, and J. Alden Weir. The layout of the house and grounds gives a sense of their artistic camaraderie. Here summers were spent sketching and painting outdoors, sitting on balconies taking in the view of the (prehighway) Strickland Brook, and eating and talking aesthetics in the common dining area. Visiting artist Elmer Livingston MacRae

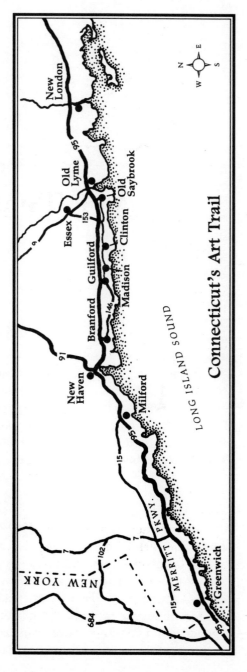

loved more than the landscape — he married the innkeeper's daughter and lived here until his death in the 1950s. His studio is re-created in a second-floor bedroom. If time allows, visit the **Bruce Museum.** The bluff-top home of textile magnate Robert Bruce has one small gallery with changing displays of Connecticut landscape paintings.

For dinner, stroll down from the inn to Greenwich Avenue, lined with fine boutiques, old-style downtown stores, and restaurants. Greenwich is unrelentingly upscale, but it's hard to fault a town that bans skateboards, in-line skates, and bicycles from the sidewalks. Right off the main street, the smartly decorated **Elm Street Oyster House** offers a number of daily fish specials as well as reliable pan-fried oysters and mini crab cakes.

Day Two

Allow at least an hour to get to **Weir Farm National Historic Site.** Drive I-95 north to exit 15, follow Route 7 north for 11 miles, turn left onto Route 102, then quickly left up Old Branchville Road. The 10 A.M. tour includes the studio of J. Alden Weir, who bought the farmstead and developed it as a painters' retreat at the turn of the century. The 153 original acres inspired hundreds of paintings and drawings by Weir and his artist friends, including Hassam, Twachtman, Albert Pinkham Ryder, and John Singer Sargent. The National Park Service acquired this site in 1990, and it's still a work in progress. Because the buildings remain occupied, the Park Service has turned to the landscape to tell Weir Farm's story. A superb walking tour of 12 spots ($2 for the brochure) lets you compare the remarkably well-preserved landscapes with the artists' conceptions.

Head back down Route 7 for seven miles, then take a left onto Route 33 to the Merritt Parkway (Route 15) east toward Milford. At Milford return to I-95 north to Branford (exit 53). Follow the Route 146 Scenic Drive east for 12 miles of salt marshes, forest, and ocean views en route to Guilford.

At the Connecticut River Museum in Essex you'll learn about the
history of the river and the landscape that inspired so many artists.
(photo by John Muldoon, courtesy Connecticut Office of Tourism)

On one edge of Guilford's scenic town green is **Cilantro,** a
coffee roaster selling fine deli sandwiches for a midday picnic. The official scenic drive ends at Route 1, but the scenery
continues. Between Madison and Clinton, turn right for
Hammonasset Beach State Park. The two-mile sandy beach
makes impressive walking, and trails crisscross the salt
marshes. Continue toward tonight's lodging in Old
Saybrook. Pocketbook allowing, the classy waterfront
Saybrook Point Inn and Spa, right at the mouth of the
Connecticut River, offers spacious, well-appointed rooms,
most with unbeatable views. A more moderate option just
off Route 1 is the **Captain Stannard House.** This circa 1850
sea captain's home has six guest rooms with lovely common
areas. Dining options include elegant seafood, meats, and
pasta at **Saybrook Point Inn's Terra Mar,** looking out on the
yacht marina, or a traditional New England shore dinner
next door at **Dock & Dine.** You could also head for the imaginative pasta and ultrafresh seafood of **Aleia's.**

Day Three

Head north five miles on Route 153 from Old Saybrook to Essex and follow Main Street to the waterfront and the **Connecticut River Museum.** Unlike most large rivers, the Connecticut does not have a major city at its mouth. As a

---

WHERE THE BIRDS ARE

The Madison Land Conservation Trust has been taking care of area natural resources since its inception in 1964. It was one of the first organizations of its kind in the country, and it continues to be a leader in environmental preservation. The MLCT has established a wonderful network of walking trails, and one of the favorites among locals is the Bailey Memorial Trail that goes along the banks of the Hammonasset River. Birders can see great blue herons, roosting owls, titmice, black-capped chickadees, blue jays, robins, phoebes, American goldfinches, white- and red-breasted nuthatches, cardinals, woodpeckers, and other birds. The scenery along this trail is spectacular, and the overlook loop at the north end has a great view of Long Island Sound. For a copy of a new guide of these trails, stop by the Audubon Shop, which in itself is a local treasure. Check here for a schedule of its weekly bird walks in Hammonasset State Park. The park has over 1,000 square acres of woodland, grassland, marsh, and seashore known as the most diverse tract of land for birding in the state — 240 different species have been spotted here.

Madison Land Conservation Trust, Inc., P.O. Box 561, Madison, CT 06443. Kirsten Livingston, secretary: 203-245-7037.

Audubon Shop, 871 Boston Post Rd., Madison (located 1½ miles west on Rte. 1 from Hammonasset State Park). Open Monday-Friday 10-6, Saturday 10-5, Sunday noon-4. 203-245-9056.

Hammonasset Beach State Park, Madison. Open Memorial Day-Labor Day 8-sunset. Connecticut vehicles $5 weekdays, $7 weekends; out-of-state vehicles $8 weekdays, $12 weekends. Before Memorial Day and after Labor Day Connecticut vehicles no charge weekdays, $5 weekends; out-of-state vehicles no charge weekdays, $7 weekends. 203-245-2785.

result, it retains healthy and undisturbed wetlands that provide a habitat to hundreds of species of wildlife. No wonder the Nature Conservancy designated it as one of the "Last Great Places." The museum focuses on the natural and human history of the river valley with ship models, prints, paintings, and shipbuilding tools. Then to brunch, or more properly the "Hunt Breakfast," at the 1776 **Griswold Inn.** This is a hearty meal to last all day, served in a cozy, low-ceilinged tavern dining room.

Return to I-95, take exit 70, and follow the signs to the **Florence Griswold Museum.** Henry Ward Ranger discovered this boardinghouse in 1899; from 1900 into the 1930s it eclipsed Cos Cob as the summer center of the American Impressionist movement. Several wall and door panels feature paintings by the boarders, including the best known of the group, William Metcalf and Childe Hassam. In Old Lyme, Hassam perfected the technique of bright and broken colors that defined the movement's style. The marshes and woods were an unending source of inspiration. If the weather's wonderful, drive the streets of Old Lyme. If you'd rather see the artists' versions, you can also drive up to New London (I-95, exit 83) to see the single gallery of Connecticut Impressionism at the **Lyman Allyn Art Museum.** When this tour is over, we guarantee you a more artistic, inspired, and passionate view of Connecticut's countryside.

– *Patricia Harris and David Lyon*

Essentials

Connecticut Impressionist Art Trail, P.O. Box 793, Old Lyme, CT 06371.

Coastal Fairfield County Convention & Visitors Bureau, 297 West Ave., Norwalk 06850. 800-866-7925, 203-899-2799.

Stanton House Inn, 76 Maple Ave., Greenwich. Double room with breakfast $89-$179. 203-869-2110.

Bush-Holley Historic House, 39 Strickland Rd., Cos Cob. Open January-March Wednesday noon-4, Saturday 11-4, Sunday 1-4; April 1-December 31 Wednesday, Thursday, Friday noon-4, Saturday 11-4, Sunday 1-4. Adults $4, seniors and students $3, under 12 free. 203-869-6899.

Bruce Museum, 1 Museum Dr., Greenwich. Open Tuesday-Saturday 10-5, Sunday 1-5. Adults $3.50, seniors and children $2.50, under 5 free, free Tuesday. 203-869-0376.

Elm Street Oyster House, 11 West Elm St., Greenwich. Open for dinner daily 5-10, Friday and Saturday 5-11. $$-$$$. 203-629-5795.

Weir Farm National Historic Site, 735 Nod Hill Rd., Wilton. Open April-November daily 8:30-5. Studio tours Wednesday-Saturday 10 A.M., walking tours Saturday and Sunday 2 P.M. 203-834-1896.

Cilantro, 85 Whitfield St., Guilford. Open daily 8-6, Sunday 8-5. 203-458-2555.

Saybrook Point Inn and Spa, 2 Bridge St., Old Saybrook. Double room $179-$275. 860-395-2000.

Captain Stannard House, 138 South Main St., Westbrook. Double room with breakfast $90-$105. 860-399-4634.

Terra Mar, at Saybrook Point Inn, 2 Bridge St., Old Saybrook. Open for dinner nightly 6-9, Saturday and Sunday 6-10. $$-$$$$. 860-395-2000.

Dock & Dine, College St., Saybrook Point, Old Saybrook. Open for dinner until 10 P.M. $$-$$$. 860-388-4665.

Aleia's, 1687 Boston Post Rd., Old Saybrook. Open for dinner Tuesday-Saturday 5:30-9, Friday and Saturday 5:30-10. $$-$$$. 860-399-5050.

Connecticut River Museum, Steamboat Dock, Essex. Open Tuesday-Sunday 10-5. Adults $4, seniors $3, children 6-12 $2, under 6 free. 860-767-8269.

Griswold Inn, 36 Main St., Essex. Sunday brunch 11-2:30. $12.95, reservations advised. 860-767-1776.

Florence Griswold Museum, 96 Lyme St., Old Lyme. Open Tuesday-Saturday 10-5, Sunday 1-5. Adults $4, seniors and students $3, under 12 free. 860-434-5542.

Lyman Allyn Art Museum, 625 Williams St., New London. Open Labor Day-June Tuesday-Sunday 1-5; July-Labor Day Tuesday-Saturday 10-5, Sunday 1-5. Adults $3, seniors and students $2, under 13 free. 860-443-2545.

Last-Minute Holiday Shopping in Litchfield

JUST AS I SHOVE AWAY THE DESSERT PLATE AT Thanksgiving, someone always brings up the "C"(Christmas) word, and I panic: Already? I haven't done any shopping. If you're like me, the solution may be to take one weekend, shop until you drop, and get it over with. This foray into the southern portion of expensive Litchfield County highlights stores with good taste and rewards you with restaurants that taste good. We keep the prices down on lodging and dining so you can hit the pricey stores for your gifts.

Day One

My top lodging choice is worth an extra drive. The **House on the Hill** is aptly named. It's in Waterbury, no one's idea of a quaint village; but this is a delightful 1888 Victorian with five comfortable rooms. Two other choices are **Merryvale** and the **Homestead Inn.** My old favorite is the **Hopkins Inn.** Its rooms run to motel decor, but they're part of a Federal-style mansion with a terrific view of Lake Waramaug.

Most shops close at 5 P.M., so arrive by early afternoon. Start in New Milford, where routes 7 and 202 part. Just off Main Street is the **Fire House on Church Street,** a store that

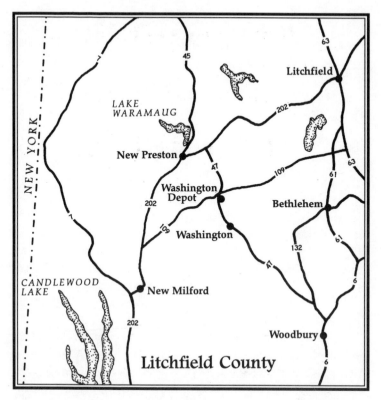

Litchfield County

features natural-fiber clothes for men, women, and children; upstairs are soaps, candles, and accessories for the home. If you need a pick-me-up, go to **Grand Patisserie** for hot chocolate and pastry. Then drive north on Route 202, watching on the left for a sign that pinpoints the right turn to the **Silo,** Ruth and Skitch Henderson's barn full of every kitchen gadget known to cooks. As I entered, a perfectly normal-looking lady, being dragged out the door bodily by her husband, was saying, "I just love this place. I could spend forever here." The Silo also runs a cooking school. Tomorrow features a marathon shopping spree, so stop now for dinner at the **Bistro,** where you can dine casually in the taproom or more formally in the upstairs restaurant; specials change nightly.

Day Two

Start in New Preston, scrunched into the notch of routes 202 and 45. Except for a pharmacy, every business seems to be an antiques store. All are open on weekends, but weekday openings are spotty. The friend who has everything might like sandalwood-scented soap from **Elysian Fields,** a shop of herbal skin-care products. Usually I prefer gifts only from places I've visited, but a trip to **J. Seitz & Co.** is as good as having been to Santa Fe. There's casual apparel along with men's flannel boxer shorts, a hand-painted "Gone Fishing" sign, chenille socks, and hand-carved santos. If one of your party starts to flag, send him (it's usually a "him" who flags first) to **Black Bear Coffee Roasters** for sweets and coffee.

When you've scoured New Preston, head north on Route 202 into Litchfield, the nerve center of Christmas Shopping Present, and park by the green to attack the town's one block of shops along West Street. **P. S. Gallery** displays artists with a connection to the Litchfield area. **Rachel's Country** carries Americana by contemporary craftspeople. The furniture is all 18th- and 19th-century at **Jeffrey Tillou Antiques** and priced accordingly. **Hayseed** sells mostly women's casual clothing — buttery leather gloves, flattering winter hats, and chenille scarves — as well as some crafts, such as carved piggy-handled salad tossers. In the cobblestone alley behind Hayseed, look for **Wildlife Landing,** which sells anything with an animal theme, including a "bubble" watch with a floating gorilla. **Troy Brook Visions Gallery,** in an old stable, showcases the work of cabinetmaker Daniel Gugnoni, just in case you decide Santa should give you an armoire for Christmas. **Kitchenworks** has a fleur-de-lis coffee set for one, among the gelatin molds and Le Creuset cookware.

Your choice for lunch in Litchfield depends on your taste. The **West Street Grill** brings SoHo to the Litchfield Hills. I had a grilled eggplant with onion and mozzarella sandwich, while the lady at the next table looked happy with her smoked turkey sandwich with cranberry relish. Nearly

The Congregational church on the green is one of the many beautiful buildings that make Litchfield a picture-perfect New England town. (photo by John Muldoon, courtesy Connecticut Office of Tourism)

next door at **Litchfield Food Company** you can also get a grilled eggplant sandwich in a more casual setting. Take care of the green thumbs on your list with gardening books and implements from the small shop of the famed **White Flower Farm.** Find it by continuing north on Route 202, then turn south on Route 63.

WHERE TO FIND JUST THE RIGHT BOOK

People who visit Whitlock Farm Booksellers in Bethany leave themselves lots of time. With an inventory of 50,000 books most folks spend the better part of the day. Whitlock's has an extensive selection of rare books, prints, maps, and military and Connecticut history, as well as books on all other subjects including popular and science fiction, some paperbacks and magazines, and postcards. Books are divided among two red barns: Those that are over $5 are in the turkey barn, and those that are under $5 are in the sheep barn. Proprietor Gilbert Whitlock has been selling books here since 1948. He says, "My father had a bookstore in New Haven in the early 1900s, and when farming got difficult, I took to selling books, too." The farm is off the beaten path; first-timers to Whitlock's often miss the right road. From Route 15, take exit 59 and turn left onto Route 69. Look for Morris Road (right before the Bethany town line), and turn left onto it. Off Morris turn right onto Sperry Road and look for the two red barns.

Whitlock Farm Booksellers, 20 Sperry Rd., Bethany, CT 06525. Open Tuesday-Sunday 9-5. 203-393-1240.

Next stop is Bethlehem, Connecticut. Take a jog southwest on Route 61 for a rolling drive with unobstructed views of 18th-century houses and red barns. At the intersection with Route 132 in the heart of Bethlehem, turn east, then look to your right for the **Christmas Shop,** a must if anyone on your list loves ornaments, entire teeny villages, angels, or every possible permutation of Santa Claus. Besides, who could resist visiting a store so fittingly located? Backtrack north to the junction with Route 109 and turn west toward Washington. This lovely Connecticut countryside is a frugal reward for hard shopping. Just when you think you need a molasses cookie and a cup of coffee, turn into Titus Square in Washington Depot and look for the **Pantry.** Don't waste a moment: You can select mugs, plates, and kitchen sundries here while you sip. End this busy day with dinner at one of

Litchfield County's most acclaimed restaurants, **Carole Peck's Good News Café.** In this cheery setting of lemon-yellow walls hung with the work of local artists, Peck delivers dinners such as wok-seared shrimp and Jack's pecan-crusted fresh oysters with aioli. On the way to the restaurant, note which antiques stores strung out along Route 6 in Woodbury you'll want to stop at tomorrow.

Day Three
Woodbury proclaims itself the state's antiques capital, and it may very well be right. Dozens of shops line Route 6 (Main Street), and a copilot to watch for signs would come in handy here. Most stores are open 10-5 at least some weekdays, noon-5 Sunday. A helpful brochure is widely available. To put it mildly, the finds here have all been found. I saw bureaus for $14,000 and a grandfather clock for $600 — the clock was eight inches high. But poking produces results. Among the gorgeous, and gorgeously priced, French armoires and tables at **Country Loft Antiques,** you might uncover Dutch tin chocolate molds or a pretty green faience jug. At **Nancy Fierberg Antiques** you might find a pair of George Washington andirons. Don't miss **Grass Roots Antiques** — whose name hints at prices that normal people can afford — for abalone salt shakers, pretty crystal liqueur glasses, or a painted glass water decanter and matching glasses, for example. It's been a rough weekend. But don't you feel better now? And it's not even December 24 yet.

– Janice Brand

E s s e n t i a l s

Litchfield Hills Travel Council, P.O. Box 968, Litchfield, CT 06759. 860-567-4506.

House on the Hill, 92 Woodlawn Terrace, Waterbury. Double room with breakfast $100-$150. 203-757-9901.

Merryvale, 1204 South Main St., Woodbury. Double room with breakfast $99-$115. 203-266-0800.

Homestead Inn, 5 Elm St., New Milford. Double room with breakfast $78-$101. 860-354-4080.

Hopkins Inn, 22 Hopkins Rd., New Preston. Double room $63-$73, no credit cards. 860-868-7295.

Fire House on Church Street, 19 Church St., New Milford. Open Monday-Saturday 9:30-5:30, Sunday 11-5. 860-355-2790.

Grand Patisserie, 27 Main St., New Milford. Open Monday 7-4, Tuesday-Friday 7-6, Saturday 8-5, Sunday 8-noon. 860-354-4525.

Silo, 44 Upland Rd., New Milford. Open daily 10-5. 860-355-0300.

Bistro, 31 Bank St., New Milford. Open for dinner nightly 5-10. $-$$. 860-355-3266.

Elysian Fields, 5 Main St., New Preston. Open Monday-Saturday 10-5, Sunday noon-5. 860-868-7711.

J. Seitz & Co., 9 East Shore Rd., New Preston. Open daily 9:30-5:30, Sunday 11-5. 860-868-0119.

Black Bear Coffee Roasters, 239 New Milford Tpke., Route 202, Marble Dale (1 mi. south of New Preston). Open daily 8-5, closed Tuesday and Wednesday. 860-868-1446.

P. S. Gallery, 41 West St., Litchfield. Open daily 11-4, closed Wednesday. 860-567-1059.

Rachel's Country, West St., Litchfield. 860-567-4282.

Jeffrey Tillou Antiques, 33 West St., Litchfield. Open daily 10:30-5, Sunday 11-4, closed Tuesday. 860-567-9693.

Hayseed, West St., Litchfield. Open Monday-Saturday 10-6, Sunday noon-6. 860-567-8775.

Wildlife Landing, Cobble Court, Litchfield. Open Monday-Saturday 10-5, Sunday 11-5. 860-567-4573.

Troy Brook Visions Gallery, 14 Cobble Court, Litchfield. Open Tuesday-Friday and Sunday noon-5, Saturday 10-5. 860-567-2310.

Kitchenworks, 23 West St., Litchfield. Open Monday-

Saturday 10-5, Sunday noon-5. 860-567-5011.

West Street Grill, 43 West St., Litchfield. Open daily for lunch 11:30-3. 860-567-3885.

Litchfield Food Company, 39 West St., Litchfield. Open for lunch every day except Wednesday. 860-567-3113.

White Flower Farm, Rte. 63, Litchfield. Open daily 10-5. 860-567-8789.

Christmas Shop, 18 East St., Bethlehem. Open Monday-Saturday 10-6, Sunday noon-5. 203-266-7048.

Pantry, Titus Sq., Washington Depot. Open Tuesday-Saturday 10-6. 860-868-0258.

Carole Peck's Good News Café, 694 Main St. S., Woodbury. Open for dinner nightly 5-10, closed Tuesday. $$$. 860-266-4663.

Country Loft Antiques, 557 Main St. S., Woodbury. Open daily 10-5, Sunday noon-5, closed Tuesday. 203-266-4500.

Nancy Fierberg Antiques, 289 Main St. S., Woodbury. Open Wednesday-Saturday 11-5, Sunday 1-5. 203-263-4957.

Grass Roots Antiques, 12 Main St. N., Woodbury. Open Tuesday-Saturday 11-5, Sunday 1-5. 203-263-3983.

A Spring Drive Along the Connecticut Coast

FROM NEW HAVEN TO GUILFORD TO NEW LONDON, there's plenty to see and do in a late spring drive along the coast. Connecticut has over 250 miles of shoreline and all of it borders Long Island Sound. Some of New England's oldest towns developed along this shore and up the Connecticut River. The villages of Connecticut's seaports offer art, architecture, and enough antiquity to satisfy the history buff in the family.

Day One

Arrive in New Haven in the afternoon to sample some of Yale University's highlights. Take I-95 exit 47 to Chapel Street via York Street. Find a parking lot (there are dozens of them) and slip on your walking shoes.

Founded in 1638, New Haven has evolved from an 18th-century West Indies trading hub to a 20th-century college town. Yale University, the nation's third oldest, is the chief attraction. At the **Yale Information Center** you can stock up on maps, museum brochures, and pamphlets or sign up for a guided campus tour.

Choose among three terrific museums. If you have children along, head for the dinosaurs at the **Peabody**

Museum of Natural History. Alternately, abandon the city pavement for the cool, pastoral landscapes of Gainsborough and Morland at the **Yale Center for British Art.** This airy museum houses the most comprehensive collection of British art outside Britain. Or across the street you can visit the **Yale University Art Gallery.** This is the oldest university art museum in North America; its nearly 100,000 works range from ancient Egyptian art to 20th-century paintings.

Take a mid-afternoon snack break at **Willoughby's Coffee and Tea,** or try the **Atticus Bookstore Café.** Spend the rest of the day cruising the stacks in New Haven's 26-plus bookstores. Pick up the *Guide to New Haven Bookshops* at Atticus or any other bookstore. For dinner remember that New Haven is famous for pizza. Try **Frank Pepe's Pizzeria Napoletana,** thought by many to serve the best thin- and chewy-crusted clam pizza around. Or stroll down Chapel Street,

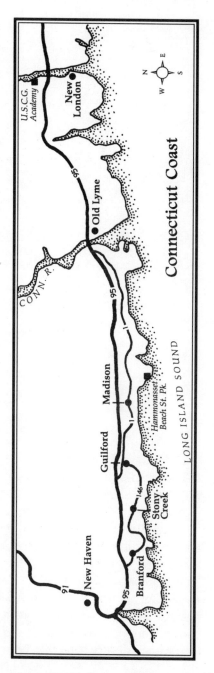

See dinosaur skeletons and the largest mural in the world depicting these giant creatures at the Peabody Museum of Natural History at Yale. (photo by John Muldoon, courtesy Connecticut Office of Tourism)

reading posted menus until you find something that strikes your fancy. Long on culture, New Haven is short on inns. The **Park Plaza** is inexpensive, serviceable, and well located. Also nearby is the **Colony Inn Hotel.**

Day Two

Breakfast early so you can be in Stony Creek for the first Thimble Island cruise at 10:20. Interstate 95 can be congested; allow an hour or more for the drive. Take exit 53 and follow the signs to Route 146 to begin a 16-mile scenic drive from Branford Center. (Look for the James Blackstone Memorial Library, the formidable Greek Revival building, on your left as you enter town.) Be patient. The first several miles wind through suburban neighborhoods, but at mile four the road turns sharply left and Long Island Sound briefly comes into view. At mile seven turn south and follow Stony Creek Road to the town dock, where several cruise lines depart on 40- to 45-minute tours of the Thimble Islands. The Thimbles are named not for their tininess as you'd suspect, but for a type of blackberry that grew here. Parking spots are scarce, so grab the first empty space. Aboard the *Sea Venture I*, Captain Dave, a garrulous fourth-generation islander, provides entertaining and educational discourse. Ask about Captain Kidd's buried treasure (as yet unfound).

After the cruise, retrace your way to Route 146 (Leetes Island Road) and continue east toward Guilford. At the intersection turn right onto Sachems Head Road (Route 146 continues to the left) to start a scenic detour past meadows, rocky fields, and ocean views. At the fork bear left onto Vineyard Point Road, then right onto Falcon Road. Turn left onto Uncas Point Road (look to your left for one last peek at the water), and right onto Old Sachems Head Road. At the intersection turn left onto Colonial Road, which brings you back to Sachems Head Road, then Route 146. Continue east on Route 146 to Guilford, a town that retains its mythic New England quality. Park on any of the streets framing the historic town green, and stop at the **Bistro on the Green** or **Cilantro** for lunch.

Spend the afternoon poking around the town, founded in 1639 by a band of English settlers. Shops of every ilk line the green, and just a mile or so away the **Guilford Handcrafts Gallery** displays and sells high-quality crafts, including pottery, fabrics, and jewelry. Or head east one town and hit the beach at **Hammonasset Beach State Park** in Madison. This is the only public beach in the area, so expect company.

For dinner, the **Place** serves seafood and corn on the cob (the best we've ever had), all roasted over an enormous outdoor barbecue pit. **Friends and Company** is an upscale family restaurant serving steaks, pasta, and seafood entrées. The homemade herb bread is wonderful.

Madison has the best lodging in the area. The **Dolly Madison Inn** inspires loyalty in its customers, some of whom have been coming for years. Down the street is the

Madison Beach Hotel, a stately Victorian on the water.

Day Three

Early risers can stroll along the water; Middle Beach West and Middle Beach Road take you there. Afterward, drive north on I-95 and take exit 70 into Old Lyme, where, if it's Sunday, you have two brunch options: the **Old Lyme Inn** or, just down the road, the **Bee and Thistle Inn.** Between the two is a late-Georgian mansion, the **Florence Griswold Museum.** At the turn of the century, Miss Griswold took in artists of the American Impressionist movement as boarders. Some of them repaid her generosity by painting some of the walls and door panels.

For another view of seaside life, continue north on I-95 to exit 83 and the **Coast Guard Academy**. Commencement is in May, so watch for crowds then. The 295-foot, square-rigged *Eagle,* a tall ship training vessel, will be receiving visitors until it departs on the summer training cruise in May, and there's your nautical end to a shoreline trip.

– Lori Baird

Essentials

Greater New Haven Convention & Visitors Bureau, 1 Long Wharf Dr., Suite 7, New Haven, CT 06511. 800-332-7829, 203-777-8550.

Connecticut River Valley & Shoreline Visitors Council, 393 Main St., Middletown, CT 06457. 800-486-3346, 860-347-0028.

Connecticut's Mystic & More, Southeastern Connecticut Tourism District, 470 Bank St., New London, CT 06320. 800-863-6569, 860-444-2206.

Yale Information Center, 149 Elm St., New Haven. Open daily 10-5, tours Monday-Friday 10:30 and 2, Saturday and Sunday 1:30. 203-432-2300.

Peabody Museum of Natural History, 170 Whitney Ave., New Haven. Open Monday-Saturday 10-5, Sunday noon-5. Adults $5, seniors and children 3-15 $3, under 3 free. 203-432-5050.

Yale Center for British Art, 1080 Chapel St., New Haven. Open Tuesday-Saturday 10-5, Sunday noon-5. 203-432-2800.

Yale University Art Gallery, 1111 Chapel St., New Haven. Open Tuesday-Saturday 10-5, Sunday 2-5, closed August. 203-432-0600.

Willoughby's Coffee and Tea, 1006 Chapel St., New Haven. Open daily 8-6. 203-789-8400.

Atticus Bookstore Café, 1082 Chapel St., New Haven. Open daily 8 A.M.-midnight. 203-776-4040.

Frank Pepe's Pizzeria Napoletana, 157 Wooster St., New Haven. Open Monday, Wednesday, Thursday 4-9:30 P.M., Friday and Saturday 11:30-11:30, Sunday 2:30-9:30 P.M., closed Tuesday. $-$$. 203-865-5762.

Park Plaza, 155 Temple St., New Haven. Double room $89. 203-865-9034.

Colony Inn Hotel, 1157 Chapel St., New Haven. Double room $109. 203-776-1234.

Sea Venture I, Stony Creek dock. Open seasonally, boards 20 past the hour 10-4. Adults $5, children under 12 $3. 203-397-3921.

Bistro on the Green, 25 Whitfield St., Guilford. Open daily 11:30-9:30, Saturday and Sunday 8:30 A.M.-9:30 P.M. 203-458-9059.

Cilantro, 85 Whitfield St., Guilford. Open daily 8-6, Sunday 8-5. 203-458-2555.

Guilford Handcrafts Gallery, 411 Church St., Guilford. Open daily 10-5, Sunday noon-4. 203-453-5947.

Hammonasset Beach State Park, Madison. Open Memorial Day-Labor Day 8 A.M.-sunset. Connecticut vehicles $5 weekdays, $7 weekends; out-of-state vehicles $8 weekdays, $12 weekends. Before Memorial Day and after Labor Day,

Connecticut vehicles no charge weekdays, $5 weekends; out-of state vehicles no charge weekdays, $7 weekends. 203-245-2785.

Place, 901 Boston Post Rd., Guilford. Open daily in season. $-$$, BYOB. 203-453-9276.

Friends and Company, 11 Boston Post Rd., Madison. Open daily for dinner Monday-Thursday 5-10, Friday and Saturday 5-11, Sunday 4:30-9. $-$$. 203-245-0462.

Dolly Madison Inn, 73 West Wharf Rd., Madison. Double room $40-$105. 203-245-7377.

Madison Beach Hotel, 94 West Wharf Rd., Madison. Double room $95-$225. 203-245-1404.

Old Lyme Inn, 85 Lyme St., Old Lyme. Sunday brunch 11-3. $$. 860-434-2600.

Bee and Thistle Inn, 100 Lyme St., Old Lyme. Sunday brunch 11-2. $$. 860-434-1667.

Florence Griswold Museum, 96 Lyme St., Old Lyme. Open Tuesday-Saturday 10-5, Sunday 1-5. Adults $4, seniors and students $3, under 12 free. 860-443-2545.

Coast Guard Academy, 15 Mohegan Ave., New London. Open daily 9-5. 860-444-8444.

Day Trip: Antiquing Your Way Through Connecticut's Quiet Corner

"SO WHERE DID YOU GO IN CONNECTICUT?" ASKED A friend over dinner when I got home. "I was in the northeast corner," I said, "in Pomfret and Woodstock and Danielson." "Never heard of 'em," she replied.

Most people have never heard of, let alone visited, what is called "the Quiet Corner," which lies between interstates 84 and 395 and north of Norwich. Too bad. Trains once brought the swells from the cities to build immense summer estates. Today, at the very least a day trip is quite worthwhile, thanks to the bucolic hilltop vistas and the current crop of antiques stores, cafés, and restaurants.

Begin this trip by taking I-395 to exit 97 for Route 44, one of the main roads in the area. It's about a half hour from Hartford or Providence, an hour from Boston, and 2½ hours from New York City. Heading west on 44, you'll be passing through Putnam, the industrial adjunct to rural Pomfret.

Here the Quinebaug River was dammed to create the power for mills and the region's early wealth.

If you're eager to start treasure hunting, stop in Putnam at **Grams & Pennyweights Antiques,** a multidealer shop that, like many in the area, is open daily. On Main Street look for **Antiques Marketplace,** where there are more than 250 dealers who offer just about anything you can think of. Don't miss the Mission furniture on the top two floors of this four-floor shop. At **G. A. Renshaw Architecturals,** housed in an old furniture store down the street, look for big architectural pieces like stained-glass windows, bars, doors, columns, and staircases. Be sure to ask here for a Putnam Antiques District map, which will lead you to most of the antiques stores and other shops in the area.

Stay on Route 44 and you quickly leave the city behind. Suddenly the landscape opens into big rolling hills punctuated with barns, farmhouses, and elegant Colonial homes. Follow the pleasantly roller-coaster road to the intersection of routes 169 and 97, then stop for lunch or a pick-me-up muffin at the family-run **Vanilla Bean Café** in Pomfret. Sandwiches are thick and fresh, best enjoyed at the counter facing a big picture window, where the sun pours in. The apple strudel, cinnamon buns, and creamy hot chocolate are addictive. This is also a good place to start your journey in the area because the café always seems to stock an ample supply of local brochures — guides to antiques and crafts, lodging, restaurants, and attractions. On weekends the café features folk and acoustic music. I know there is no way you are hungry now, but if you are planning to stay in the area for dinner, make a note of the **Harvest** (on the previous block), named in *Connecticut Magazine* as "best new restaurant" and also known for having the best brunch in Windham County. The huge circa 1765 building on Route 44 has undergone extensive renovations and is just lovely. In the cottage on the property you'll find **Wilson Campbell, Ltd.,** whose small shop features antiques, gifts, and fine works by American artisans.

Find treasures galore in the antiques shops that abound in northeast Connecticut. (photo by John Muldoon, courtesy Connecticut Office of Tourism)

For more antiques, head south on Route 169; at the light at the bottom of the hill turn right on Route 101 west. In 60 yards look for **Pomfret Antique World** on the left. Its logo, "something for everyone," couldn't be truer. Wander 15,000 square feet with 90 dealers of, well, by the looks of things, just about everything possible. Even if you don't come away with anything you need, it's fun to look — and to know someone else has to dust all this stuff.

Now to South Woodstock up Route 169, recently officially recognized as a "scenic road." It is, too. In New England tradition, Woodstock is, in reality, South Woodstock, West Woodstock, and Woodstock Valley, but most of the interest centers along this road. Look for **Scranton's Shops,** a former blacksmith shop now filled with antiques, crafts, and collectibles. Up the hill behind Scranton's is **Fox Hunt Farms Gourmet & Café,** just in case you haven't had enough coffee, homemade chocolate, or pastries yet. Even if you have, do stop here at least to buy a jar of the locally made Woodstock Hill Preserves (my favorite is raspberry jam with peaches).

Continuing south on Route 198, turn left onto Route 44. If you're in the mood for a scenic diversion, turn right onto Route 97 into Hampton. Incorporated in 1786, this is a New England town that looks just like a New England town should.

A bit east of Hampton, you'll find Danielson. Finish the trip with a stop here at **Logee's Greenhouses.** From Route 101, turn right on Maple Street, then left onto North Street. Since William D. Logee opened the greenhouse in 1892, the Logees have cultivated this warm oasis, specializing in begonias, bougainvillea, camellia, hibiscus, jasmine — the list goes on. You'll find lots of other tropical plants (grown mostly for houseplants). Even if you've packed your car with treasures, I know you'll find room for a little something from Logee's.

– Janice Brand

Essentials

Northeast Connecticut Visitors District, P.O. Box 598, Putnam, CT 06260. 860-928-1228.

Grams & Pennyweights Antiques, 626 School St., Rte. 44, Putnam. Open weekdays except Tuesday 10-4, Saturday and Sunday 10-5. 860-928-6624.

Antiques Marketplace, 109 Main St., Putnam. Open daily 10-5. 860-928-0442.

G. A. Renshaw Architecturals, 75-83 Main St. Putnam. Open Wednesday-Sunday 10-5. 860-928-1905.

Vanilla Bean Café, corner of rtes. 44, 169, and 97, Pomfret. Open Monday and Tuesday 7-3, Wednesday and Thursday 7 A.M.-8 P.M., Friday and Saturday 7 A.M.-11 P.M. or until entertainment is finished. 860-928-1562.

Harvest, 37 Putnam Rd. (Rte. 44), Pomfret. Open for lunch and dinner Monday-Friday, Saturday dinner only 5:30-9:30, Sunday brunch 11-2 and dinner 2:30-7:30. $-$$$. 860-928-0008.

Wilson Campbell, Ltd., 20 Woodstock Rd., Pomfret (in the cottage at the Harvest). Open daily except Tuesday 11-5, Sunday noon-5. 860-928-1514.

Pomfret Antique World, junction rtes. 44 and 101, Pomfret Center. Open every day except Wednesday 10-5. 860-928-5006.

Scranton's Shops, 300 Rte. 169, South Woodstock. Open daily 11-5. 860-928-3738.

Fox Hunt Farms Gourmet & Café, 292 Rte. 169, South Woodstock. Open Tuesday-Sunday 10-5:30. 860-928-0714.

Logee's Greenhouses, 141 North St., Danielson. Open Monday-Saturday 9-4, Sunday 11-4. 860-774-8038.

Rhode Island

Perfect Providence Weekend

THERE ARE TWO THINGS YOU NEED FOR A SUCCESSFUL weekend in Providence: a big appetite and a map. You need the first because the city is ripe with great restaurants. You need the second because it's very hard to find a map of Providence in Providence. The reason you'll want a map is so that you can find downtown (tall office buildings, the Providence Biltmore, Weybosset and Westminster streets, the Arcade) and the East Side (Colonial houses, College Hill, Benefit Street, Brown University, Rhode Island School of Design). This, then, is a weekend devoted to the art of eating, the art of Providence (museums and galleries), and the art of trying to get from Point A to Point B.

Day One

You can arrive by train, although driving into and around the city is not nearly the nightmare that it is in Boston. Check with Amtrak for trains and fares. Otherwise, drive in on I-95. For overnighting, the best for location and amenities is the 219-room **Providence Biltmore.** The brick facade and lobby's gilt ceiling recall the hotel's grand 1922 opening. For more intimate surroundings, the ten-room **Old Court** offers Victorian decor and a flavor of Providence's toniest address — Benefit Street. Other B&Bs are springing up; call the **Greater Providence Convention and Visitors Bureau** office for more particulars, or get their map of Providence, the "Banner Trail."

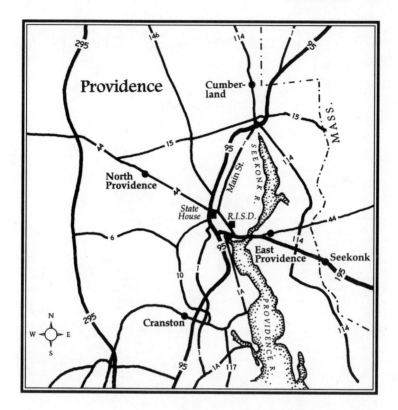

Check into your accommodations, then find your way to dinner at **New Rivers**. Old-timers will recognize the address as Al Forno's former digs. The black-and-purple color scheme has given way to serene hunter green and terra cotta, but it's still teensy, with only about 12 tables. If the Providence salad of summer-fresh greens is on New Rivers's menu, don't pass it by. Likewise the Vietnamese sampler — skewered chicken marinated with five-spice powder, coconut milk, and brown sugar, then grilled, and wrappers of vegetables and shrimp to dunk into a spicy sauce. Risotto, studded with chicken and asparagus, had just the right bite to it; a veal T-bone with mashed potatoes, sautéed zucchini, and red cabbage filled the biggest plate I have ever seen. Welcome to the Providence Portion: Chefs in this city must

Waterplace Park, set around a tidal basin, has an amphitheater, landscaped terraces, and water taxis that carry visitors south to Main Street attractions. (photo by Jim McElholm, courtesy Providence Convention and Visitors Bureau)

live in fear that patrons will die of hunger if not served Brobdingnagian portions. At New Rivers, modest eaters can make a meal of a sampler or by sharing an entrée; gour-

mands will be sated at last. Hats off to chefs Bruce and Pat
Tillinghast for their wide-ranging experiments.

Day Two

Today you'll be able to walk off all you ate last night. If
you're a morning person, head for downtown's Westminster
Street to stroll its quiet blocks. Look above the modern storefronts to see the handsome Victorian commercial buildings.
Benefit Street gets all the attention for architecture, but I
think downtown's stolid brick, fanciful stone, and art deco
buildings are just as deserving. Between Westminster and
Weybosset sits the Arcade, touted as the country's first
"mall," a handsome 1828 building that opens to a three-story
gallery of balustrades and marble floors. The first floor is full
of food concessions and tables of people watchers. Among
the second-floor boutiques is **Copacetic,** for handmade jewelry, clocks, lasers, and other interesting gifts, and a bookshop where you can buy the hard-to-read but detailed *Arrow
Map of Greater Providence* ($2.50).

Plan to join the slugabeds at 10:30 at the **Museum of
Art at the Rhode Island School of Design.** This is the perfect weekend museum: In about two hours you can comfortably see the entire collection, which ranges from Nesmin, an
Egyptian mummy, to Monets and Picassos. Part of the museum, the Pendleton House, was designed to display a collection of American furniture in period setting, so that after
wandering through Impressionist art or Japanese textiles,
you'll turn a corner into an 18th-century Colonial parlor.

Hungry? Climb College Hill, heading up Angell Street,
to take a left on Thayer, the commercial center of Brown
University. The stores appeal mostly to the young, but the
bookstores will interest anyone with an inquiring mind. But
browse after lunch: Just behind the CVS is **Adesso.** Enjoy
skylights and large expanses of glass and Providence Portion
pastas and salads, wood-fired pizza, and grilled items.
Fortified, devote the afternoon to exploring architecture and

steep streets. Wend your way to Benefit Street, at the base of the hill, which presents a wall of historic houses reminiscent of both Nantucket and Cambridge's Brattle Street. Stop by the **Providence Athenaeum,** one of the country's oldest subscription libraries, or head for the **RISD Store** to browse for art books or art supplies.

After a rest, dine tonight at **Al Forno,** where Providence's culinary style was perfected. No reservations are taken, so dine early or late to avoid long waits. Chef-owners George Germon and Johanne Killeen have achieved national fame for their Providence Portions of signature free-form grilled pizzas and elegant pastas such as roasted asparagus under a blanket of pasta with Parmesan and butter, served amid creaky chairs and wood tables in an old converted stable. If you don't want another big meal, retreat to the reliably French coziness downstairs at **Pot au Feu** for a salad, quiche, and pommes frites — a sensible alternative to the Providence Portion.

Day Three

If you do want brunch out, try **Plaza Grille,** a sort of casual, upscale bistro off Atwells Avenue in Providence's Italian neighborhood. If you want to be gentle to yourself and your pocketbook, the **Downcity Diner** is the real thing. You might be able to secure aisle seats at the renowned **Trinity Repertory Company.** If not, tour the **John Brown House,** an elegant mansion off Benefit Street that houses furnishings and traces the history of Providence. Or just wander around College Hill's art galleries: **Woods-Gerry Gallery,** where RISD faculty and students display their works in a 19th-century mansion designed by Richard Upjohn (who designed New York City's Trinity Church), and the two galleries in the **Providence Art Club** — an artful end to your weekend.

— Janice Brand

THE BEST ETHNIC MARKETS

Barbara Kuck, director of the Culinary Archives & Museum at Johnson & Wales University, really knows her way around the unsung ethnic markets, bakeries, delis, and ladle houses of Providence. Vietnamese, Salvadoran, Russian, Portuguese, Italian — all of it is here within a 15-minute drive from downtown. She says Broad Street (Latin on one end, Asian on the other) is the ethnic heart of the city, but Atwells Avenue on Federal Hill (the little Italy of Providence) is not to be missed either. For a complete guide to ethnic food in Providence, stop at the museum. Here is a handful of Barbara's favorites.

Culinary Archives & Museum at Johnson & Wales University, 315 Harborside Blvd., Providence. 401-598-2805. There are plans to move to a new building in the near future, so be sure to call ahead.

Portuguese American Market, 896 Allens Ave., Providence. 401-941-4480. Can't go wrong with these breads, *palitos de cintra,* sweet lemony dunkers for coffee, and coconut and citrus tartlets.

Near East Market, 602 Reservoir Ave., Cranston. 401-941-9763. Creamy Bulgarian ground-lamb pizzas known as *lahmejun* and enormous wheels of cracker bread.

Ursula's European Pastries, 1860 Broad St., Cranston. Barbara (a former pastry chef) recommends the Hungarian *dobos torte,* but everything here is outstanding.

La Famosa, 1035 Broad St., Providence. 401-941-4550. Ask for the toasted coconut macaroons.

Sanchez Market, 676 Broad St., Providence. 401-831-5470. Sells everything from fresh aloe and codfish fritter mix to extractors for sugarcane juice.

Wing Kee, 312 Broad St., Providence. 401-751-8688. Simon Chan and his wife, Sandy, have been barbecuing ducks for 17 years. Don't miss these succulent birds.

Asian Bakery & Fast Food, 310 Broad St., Providence. 401-421-6920. A sure bet is *bahn bao,* a savory rice-flour dumpling filled with pork and hard-boiled egg and Saigon sandwiches: pâté, roast pork, slivered carrots, fish sauce, and cilantro on crisp French bread.

Antonelli's Poultry Co., 62 DePasquale Square, Providence. 401-421-8739. So authentic is this shop filled with live geese, ducks, rabbits, and chickens that the butcher will slaughter to order.

Providence Cheese and Tavola Calda, 178 Atwells Ave., Providence. 401-421-5653. Here you can mix and match pastas and fillings to order. Try red-pepper ravioli stuffed with spinach ricotta.

Barbara also recommends the shops on Atwells Avenue on Federal Hill (the Little Italy of Providence).

Essentials

Greater Providence/Warwick Convention and Visitors Bureau, 1 West Exchange St., Providence 02903. 800-233-1636, 401-274-1636.

Providence Biltmore, Kennedy Plaza. Double room $130-$170. 800-294-7709, 401-421-0700.

Old Court, 144 Benefit St. Double room with breakfast $90-$135. 401-751-2002.

New Rivers, 7 Steeple St. Open for dinner Tuesday-Saturday 5:30-10. $$-$$$. 401-751-0350.

Copacetic, 65 Weybosset St. Open Monday-Friday 10-7, Saturday 10-6, Sunday noon-5. 401-273-0470.

Museum of Art, Rhode Island School of Design, 224 Benefit St. Open Wednesday-Sunday 10-5, Friday 10-8. Adults $5, seniors $4, college students $2, children 5-18 $1, under 5 free. 401-454-6100.

Adesso, 161 Cushing St. Open for lunch Tuesday-Saturday 11:45-2:30, pizza and cold salads 2:30-5. $$-$$$. 401-521-0770.

Providence Athenaeum, 251 Benefit St. Open fall, winter, and spring Monday-Friday 8:30-5:30, Saturday 9:30-5:30, Sunday 1-5. 401-421-6970.

RISD Store, 30 North Main St. Open Monday-Friday 8:30-6:30, Saturday 10-6, Sunday noon-5. 401-454-6465.

Al Forno, 577 South Main St. Open for dinner Tuesday-Friday 5-10, Saturday 4-10. $$$-$$$$. 401-273-9760.

Pot au Feu, 44 Custom House St. Open for dinner Monday-Thursday 5:30-9, Friday and Saturday 5:30-11. $$-$$$. 401-401-273-8953.

Plaza Grille, 64 DePasquale Plaza. Open for brunch Saturday and Sunday 8:30-2:30. $. 401-274-8684.

Downcity Diner, 151 Weybosset St. Open for brunch Saturday and Sunday 9-2. $. 401-331-9217.

Trinity Repertory Company, 201 Washington St. 401-351-4242.

John Brown House, 52 Power St. Open Tuesday-Saturday 10-5, Sunday noon-4. Adults $6. 401-331-8575.

Woods-Gerry Gallery, 62 Prospect St. Open Monday-Saturday 10-4, Sunday 2-5. 401-454-6100, ext. 6141.

Providence Art Club, 11 Thomas St. Open Monday-Friday 11-4, Saturday noon-3, Sunday 3-5. 401-331-1114.

Vineyards and Views in a Bit of Massachusetts and Rhode Island

*THE EASTERN EDGE OF RHODE ISLAND AND THE SOUTH-*eastern wedge of Massachusetts present miles of pastureland sloping down to the sea, offering wild and unspoiled vistas more typical of Ireland than of New England. In the industrial cities of Fall River and New Bedford, as well as in the pretty harbors and handsome weathered houses of small coastal villages, are veins that run deep with shipbuilding and whaling history.

Day One

Start your tour before lunch if you can, in Little Compton, Rhode Island, which belonged to Massachusetts in 1746. Here is serene country of windswept ocean views, green fields, and a quilt work of what might be the most artistically and solidly built stone walls left in one New England place. To get there, take Route 195 east from Providence, then Route 24 south from Fall River. Exit at Main Road and turn left, bringing you into Tiverton Four Corners. Lay in some gourmet picnic fixings at **Provender Fine Foods.** The ideal

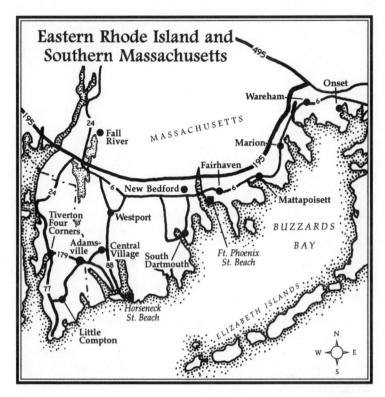

Eastern Rhode Island and Southern Massachusetts

picnic spot on a hot August afternoon lies among the fragrant rows of grapes, landscaped with daylilies, at **Sakonnet Vineyards.** Buy a cold bottle of wine to go with your lunch, perhaps Eye of the Storm or America's Cup White. (The tour is interesting, too.)

From Sakonnet Vineyards head east to Adamsville, site of the world's only monument to a chicken — the Rhode Island Red — at the intersection of Main Road and Harbor Road. From there take Adamsville Road east to Central Village. Then turn right on Main Road in Westport. This route meanders through cornfields and pasturelands, around the Westport River's east branch. Once the cornfields thin out, you'll start seeing shingle and clapboard houses with neatly lettered wooden signs ("William and Samuel Brightman, Mariners, ca. 1788/1830"; "Abner Sisson,

Housewright, ca. 1841"). You'll be in Westport Point, where a surprising number of 18th- and 19th-century houses of merchants and mariners survive. Lining the narrow street, set tidily behind white picket fences, these houses have such distinctive Federal details as fluted pilasters and carved door pediments. Route 88 south ends at the flat peninsula that is Horseneck Beach State Reservation, a two-mile-long barrier beach with bathhouses to accommodate swimmers.

The next stop is the **Lloyd Center for Environmental Studies,** with its exhibits devoted to the coastal and estuarine natural history of Buzzards Bay. A third-floor observation room offers mesmerizing views of Buzzards Bay and the Elizabeth Islands. Call well ahead to stay in South Dartmouth at **Salt Marsh Farm** — it has only two rooms. A surer bet is in Fairhaven at the **Edgewater B&B,** which is a far handier place to stay for exploring New Bedford than New Bedford itself. For dinner, New Bedford offers only slim pickings. But Westport and South Dartmouth have lots more dining choices.

Day Two

Before leaving Fairhaven, visit Fort Phoenix State Beach (down Green Street off Route 6). Here you'll find a narrow beach and a cannon-braced Revolutionary War fort that withstood a British invasion. A long paved dike leads out to a pair of giant, curved hurricane gates (85 feet tall) that can be closed to protect New Bedford harbor against flooding. The rest of the day will be devoted to exploring downtown New Bedford, a mine of whaling history. From the Edgewater B&B take Route 195 and the Route 18 downtown exit. First drive a few blocks west of the historic district to see the **Rotch-Jones-Duff House and Garden Museum,** a gorgeous yellow Greek Revival mansion that was home to two whaling merchants and an industrialist. Call ahead to find out about special events. Head to **Freestone's** for lunch, and afterward, stroll over to Fishermen's Wharf to see the fishing fleet, one of the East Coast's largest.

Then make your way to the **New Bedford Whaling Museum.** Plan on a couple of hours to see the Herman Melville memorabilia, scrimshaw gadgets, dramatic paintings of whales biting dories in half, and the Mount Washington Art Glass once made in New Bedford. Clambering aboard the half-scale replica of the whale ship *Lagoda* gives you a little feel for the whaling life. Across the street is the Seamen's Bethel, a somber spot famed for its pulpit shaped like a ship's prow. It was described by Melville in *Moby-Dick*.

Before dinner, check into the **Onset Pointe Inn,** a rambling Victorian mansion set on the beach in the village of Onset. Sea views and sunlight suffuse every room, from wicker-furnished sunporch to spacious, antiques-filled guest rooms. When you sit up in bed, your elbows almost brush the ocean.

The arcadelike character of Route 6 in Wareham foretells

WHERE TO GET THE RIGHT CORNMEAL FOR JOHNNYCAKES

Little Compton claims the biggest winery in New England, the biggest potato harvest in Rhode Island, and one of the oldest gristmills in the United States — Gray's Grist Mill. On most days you can find miller Tim McTague pouring a bushel of whitecap flint corn into the hopper to mill a batch of johnnycake meal. Two giant stones — 15 inches thick and weighing a ton each — grind the corn into meal. Tim lets the meal fall from the chute through his fingers, testing the consistency. He knows at a touch whether the texture will work for johnnycakes. Rhode Islanders know that true johnnycakes are made from whitecap flint corn ground between granite millstones. To order stone-ground johnnycake meal and other flours by mail, contact: **Gray's Grist Mill,** P.O. Box 422, Adamsville, RI 02801. 508-636-6075 (don't worry about the Massachusetts area code — this is the right number!).

the evening's dining expectations. Although it's sort of a blend of roller derby and dining factory, **Lindsey's Restaurant** puts out some of the freshest and best seafood around: more than two dozen seafood dishes cooked four different ways, as well as other traditional Yankee fare, and outstanding homemade desserts.

Day Three

If you have taken your inn breakfast out to the porch, you may be tempted to laze on the beach the rest of the day. Nothing wrong with that. From the small strip of beach, you can regard Onset Bay and tiny Wickets Island, rumored to be for sale for about $3 million. Those with any initiative left should head for the attractive and historic waterfronts of Marion and Mattapoisett, both reached via Route 6. Both towns have a Water Street: Marion's leads to enormous Victorian summer haunts; Mattapoisett's to beautifully preserved 18th- and 19th-century houses set close together. Mattapoisett built more whale ships than any other port, including the ship *Acushnet* on which Herman Melville crewed. Good choices for lunch in Mattapoisett include the inexpensive takeout seafood at the **Oxford Creamery** and the **Mattapoisett Inn,** an old seaside inn.

There's probably no better way to end your afternoon than on the deck of a cruise ship traversing the Cape Cod Canal. A three-hour **Sunday Jazz Cruise** leaves the Onset town pier at 1:30 P.M. A guide points out such sites as the location of President Grover Cleveland's summer White House, Gray Gables. On the pier you can't fail to notice Kenny's Saltwater Taffy, makers of sugared popcorn bars since the 1890s. Go ahead, ruin your dinner. From Wareham pick up either Route 3 or Route 495 back to Boston, or take Route 195 back to Providence.

– *Patricia Mandell*

Essentials

Provender Fine Foods, 3883 Main Rd., Tiverton. Open Tuesday-Sunday 9-5. 401-624-8084

Sakonnet Vineyards, 162 West Main Rd., Little Compton. Open daily 10-6, tours Wednesday-Sunday 11-5. 401-635-8486.

Lloyd Center for Environmental Studies, 430 Potomska Rd., South Dartmouth. Open Tuesday-Sunday and Monday holidays 9-5. 508-990-0505.

Salt Marsh Farm, 322 Smith Neck Rd., South Dartmouth. Double room with breakfast $85-$95. 508-992-0980.

Edgewater B&B, 2 Oxford St., Fairhaven. Double room with continental breakfast $70-$95. 508-997-5512.

Bristol County Convention & Visitors Bureau, 70 North Second St., New Bedford, MA 02741. 508-997-1250.

Rotch-Jones-Duff House and Garden Museum, 396 County St., New Bedford. Open daily 10-4. Adults $4, children under 12 $1. 508-997-1401.

Freestone's, 41 Williams St., New Bedford. Open Monday-Thursday 11-11, Friday and Saturday 11 A.M.-midnight, Sunday noon-10. 508-993-7477.

New Bedford Whaling Museum, 18 Johnny Cake Hill, New Bedford. Open Memorial Day-Labor Day daily 9-5, Thursday 9-8. Adults $4.50, seniors $3.50, children 6-14 $3, under 6 free. 508-997-0046.

Onset Pointe Inn, 9 Eagle Way, Onset. Double room with breakfast $85-$175. 508-295-8442.

Lindsey's Restaurant, 3138 Cranberry Hwy., Buzzards Bay. Open daily 11:30-9. $-$$$. 508-759-5544.

Oxford Creamery, Marion Rd. and Rte. 6, Mattapoisett. Open seasonally. $. 508-758-3847.

Mattapoisett Inn, 13 Water St., Mattapoisett. Open for lunch Monday-Saturday 11:30-3:30, Sunday brunch 10:30-1:30. $. 508-758-4922.

Sunday Jazz Cruise, town pier, Onset. Seasonally at 1:30 P.M. Sundays, adults $12, children $6. 508-295-3883.

From Simple to Sumptuous: Watch Hill to Newport

LITTLE RHODIE HAS A WAY OF ALWAYS GETTING THE fuzzy end of the lollipop. Because the American mind often equates size with grandeur, this tiny chunk wedged between Massachusetts and Connecticut tends to be over-looked. Its 48 miles north to south seem skimpy, but venture up the coast of the Ocean State and discover more than 400 miles of scenic coastline with over 100 public beaches, about 18,000 acres devoted to parks, and 20 percent of the Registered Historic Landmarks in the United States. And of course, there's Newport, the once and present home of the nabobs, erstwhile home of the America's Cup, and present-day site of an annual international jazz festival. Not bad for a state the size of a typical county in Montana. This three-day itinerary, winding up the coast for one day and lingering in Newport for two, should show you that, yes, good things do come in small packages.

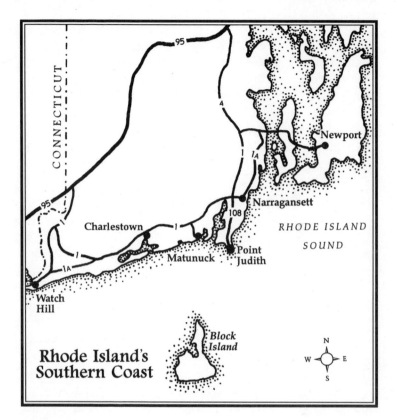

Rhode Island's Southern Coast

Day One

Start at the southwestern edge of the state in Watch Hill, aiming for Narragansett for lunch and arriving in Newport in time for dinner. The nonstop trek takes only about 45 minutes, but planned delays make for a delightful day. The quiet little seaside town of Watch Hill (exit 1 off I-95) is named for its elevated vantage point and the granite watchtower that signaled ships during the French and Indian and Revolutionary wars. As a resort, it dates to the 1850s, around the same time its landmark Flying Horse Carousel was being assembled back in Germany. Plan to arrive in time for breakfast at the **Olympia Tea Room** on Bay Street, across from the main parking lot toward the middle of the three-block-long town center. The tables on the sidewalk terrace offer a generous dose of sea air and a harbor view.

After breakfast make a brief reconnaissance of Bay Street. On the harbor side a bronze figure of Indian chief Ninigret, the town guardian, brandishes two salmon. The statue was commissioned in Paris, where an Indian from Buffalo Bill's Wild West Show served as the model. In the **Book and Tackle Shop** across the street, a pair of dusty corridors is filled with books on everything from Freud to fishing, from 1940s *Life* magazines to extinct advertising posters. At the end of Bay Street whirls the Flying Horse Carousel, abandoned by a traveling carnival in 1879. Legend has it that one of the carnival's real horses was so devoted to the carousel that he refused to leave and took up residence beside his spinning friend. When the horse died, his tail was incorporated into one of the carved horses' tails. Today the locals brag that the Flying Horse is the nation's oldest, waging war with those on Martha's Vineyard, whose carousel also vies for the title. The debate goes in circles, but the expressions on the faces of children whirling past show that they couldn't care less.

Before leaving Watch Hill, drive up Bluff Avenue to pay homage to the town's grande dame, the Ocean House Hotel, an impressive yellow Victorian built in 1868. The beloved hotel has supplied Watch Hill adolescents with summer jobs for generations and was a traditional wedding and cotillion site for the community. The land just next to the hotel was home to Chief Ninigret. Stroll the terrace and you just may decide to spend your next vacation here. From Watch Hill take Scenic 1A (Boston Neck Road) north. If a dip suits your fancy, plunge into the three-acre spring-fed swimming pond at **Ninigret Park** in Charlestown. But if your vacation could not be complete without a mood crystal, antique gown, fake-fur gorilla costume, or inflatable Godzilla, pass the park and head to the **Umbrella Factory,** a farmlike cluster of shops just a few hundred yards away.

Return to Route 1A, which leads into Route 1, until a

sign announces Matunuck and **Theatre-by-the-Sea.** Newport is only 20 minutes away, so if you want to pick up tickets for an evening show, follow the signs. Otherwise, continue north on Route 1; turn south onto Route 108 to Point Judith, the site of the rocky foundation for the lighthouse in Narragansett but better known these days as the ferry landing for the ship to Block Island.

Continue up the coast on Ocean Road/Route 1A, where entrances to driveways hint of castles beyond. Still in the town of Narragansett, you'll encounter a mammoth stone structure arching over the road ahead. Inside the curve of the archway is a tourist information center. The folks inside will tell you that the structure is the remaining skeleton of the Narragansett Pier Casino, built in 1884 and destroyed by fire in 1900. The towers are open to the public. You can stop for lunch next door at the **Coast Guard House Restaurant.** Climb the stairs to the terrace for steamed clams, Rhode Island clam chowder, and corn on the cob.

Next stop is the **South County Museum,** off Route 1A. The museum of local Colonial-era life is housed in a large barn. Exhibits include a cobbler's shop, a gentleman's study, and treasures from grandmother's sewing box. On the museum grounds is Canonchet Farm, where a Narragansett Indian named Sachem Canonchet once had his abode.

Back on Route 1 north, follow the signs to Newport. Lodging in Newport ranges from elegant to simple. The **Castle Hill Inn and Resort** is a Victorian mansion on Ocean Drive. Nearby, the palatial **Oceancliff Resort** was built to mimic an Irish castle; if your budget is tight, ask about the humble attic rooms that were once servants' quarters. Other honorable mentions include **Cliff Walk Manor,** on the Cliff Walk with a view of the beach, and the **Hotel Viking,** in the center of town. Also there are more than 60 bed-and-breakfasts you can contact through **Bed & Breakfast, Newport; Bed & Breakfast Registry at Newport;** and **Newport Historic Inns.** For dinner, among traditional favorites is the **White Horse Tavern,** which claims to be the oldest tavern in the country, on the corner of Marlborough and Farewell streets. After dinner, strolling Thames Street is de rigueur.

Day Two

Today is devoted to exploring the summer "cottages" of the once rich and famous, as well as to taking a closer look at the buildings maintained by the **Preservation Society of Newport.** But first, breakfast. On a fine Sunday we recommend the brunch at the Castle Hill Inn and Resort, where outside tables overlook a rolling lawn, the Newport Bridge in the distance, and of course, the water. Less expensive — much less, in fact — is the **Franklin Spa,** a local hangout where you can chat with the natives or sit in a booth and read the morning paper. Over breakfast, decide which mansions you'd like to tour. There are about a dozen; eight are maintained by the Preservation Society. Tickets, available at the houses and at the **Visitors Center** on America's Cup Avenue, range from $6.50 to $10 for one house to $35.50 for the eight houses run by the Preservation Society.

I don't recommend doing more than three this morning — each tour takes from 45 minutes to an hour, and all that glitters can become tiring. Among the choices: The Breakers, designed for Cornelius Vanderbilt, is the largest; the Elms, modeled after a French château, boasts a sunken garden with a rare collection of trees and shrubs; Rosecliff, with its heart-shaped staircase and gardens, was featured in the film *The Great Gatsby;* Château-sur-Mer's mirrored ballroom seems like a good party spot, too; and Marble House, built in 1892 for William K. Vanderbilt, was called the "sumptuous palace by the sea." The list goes on, but whichever other ones you visit, the Astors' Beechwood on Bellevue Avenue is a must. Though not the most impressive of the mansions architecturally, its talented young docents make it worth the while. Their playful chatter takes you back to the era of the wealthy "four hundred" who summered here throughout the 19th century.

Let the costumed "servants" at the Astors' Beechwood mansion entertain you with stories of the rich and famous of Newport society.
(courtesy Astors' Beechwood)

For lunch try **Poor Richard's** on Thames Street, where patrons sit in converted church pews and order well-stacked sandwiches. After carrot cake, head to the Treadway Inn Marina on the harbor for a one-hour harbor tour on the *Spirit of Newport.* Onboard, the wry-humored skipper gives a synopsis of Newport history and tells who owns which mansions. He'll point out the ground the Kennedys walk on, the water under which is a marine park, and the dock where Mia Farrow smooched with Robert Redford for the making of *The Great Gatsby.*

Get your land legs back by wandering the wharf area. If you are susceptible to chocolate cravings, grab a "brook-ie," a decadent brownie-cookie combo with walnuts, at the **Cookie Jar** on Bowen's Wharf. If you happen to have a photo of your favorite building (along with about $4,000 to spend), **Miniature Occasions and Dolls** will produce a teensy replica.

Do some armchair traveling at the **Armchair Sailor Bookstore** on Lee's Wharf, where you can find that glow-in-the-dark celestial map you've been searching for. Finally, look for an original print of Bugs Bunny at the **Animation Art Gallery.** For dinner, try to reserve a window table at the **Mooring,** overlooking yachts in the harbor. Seafood reigns, but the two-inch-thick slabs of steak are worth taking a stab at.

Day Three

Today is a day of walking, around town and on the ocean's edge. Start the day with breakfast at **Muriel's,** on the corner of Spring and Touro streets, where you can opt for the Belgian waffle topped with lemon whipped cream. Wooden booths and white lace curtains make for a New Englandy decor, except for the plastic mannequins smiling at you from all corners. Yes, human-sized Barbies — we meant to ask our waitress why, but got sidetracked by French toast with mapled walnuts.

After exploring Spring Street's antiques stores, head up Touro Street. You'll pass an unremarkable mauvish-beige building standing askew behind a wrought-iron fence. This is the **Touro Synagogue,** built in 1763, making it the oldest temple in America. The building stands at an angle because it faces toward Jerusalem, as is the traditional rule for Orthodox synagogues. A guide gives talks regularly (10-4 in summer) about the building and the original Jews who were drawn to Newport by its religious tolerance. At number 82 Touro is the **Newport Historical Society,** where you can join an architectural walking tour at ten o'clock on Friday and Saturday mornings.

For lunch, **Salas' Restaurant** serves clam bake, scallops, and baked cod. Or return to the wharf for clam chowder or chili and the best people watching in town at the **Black Pearl's Outdoor Café** on Bannister's Wharf. However, avoid this busy intersection of visitors if you don't like a crowd or a wait. After lunch, put on your sneakers to tackle the Cliff

Walk, the three-mile path that begins just west of Newport Beach at Memorial Boulevard and ends on a side street off Bellevue Avenue. The last part is pretty tricky and even downright dangerous in places. Let your instincts tell you when to turn back.

End the day with a sunset stroll on the beach. First Beach is the closest to Newport, Third Beach is the farthest, and yes, there's a Second Beach in between. (All charge for parking.)

— *Tanya Tabachnikoff*

Essentials

Rhode Island Tourism Division, R.I. Economic Development Corp., 1 West Exchange St., The Westin Hotel, Providence, RI 02903. 800-556-2484, 401-277-2601.

South County Tourism Council, 4808 Tower Hill Rd., Wakefield, RI 02979. 800-548 4662, 401-789-4422.

Newport County Convention & Visitors Bureau, 23 America's Ave., Newport, RI 02840. 800-976-5122, 401-849-8048.

Olympia Tea Room, 74 Bay St., Watch Hill. Open for breakfast daily 8-11:30. 401-348-8211.

Book and Tackle Shop, Bay St., Watch Hill. 401-596-1770.

Ninigret Park, Charlestown. 322-0450.

Umbrella Factory, 4820 Old Post Rd., Charlestown. Open seasonally 10-6 daily. 401-364-6616.

Theatre-by-the-Sea, 364 Card's Pond Rd., Matunuck. Open May 26-September 13, tickets $26-$28. 401-782-8587.

Coast Guard House Restaurant, 40 Ocean Rd., Narragansett. Open for lunch Monday-Saturday 11:30-3, Sunday brunch 10-3. $. 401-789-0700.

South County Museum, Rte. 1A, Canonchet Farm, Narragansett. Open May 1-October 31 Wednesday-Sunday 11-5; July-August daily 10-5, Wednesday 10-7, closed Monday. Adults $3.50, children $1.75, families $10. 401-783-5400.

Castle Hill Inn and Resort, Ocean Dr., Newport. Double room $95-$325. 888-466-1355, 401-849-3800.

Oceancliff Resort, Ridge Rd., Newport. Double room $95-$300. 401-847-7777.

Cliff Walk Manor, 82 Memorial Blvd., Newport. Double room $95-$225. 401-847-1300.

Hotel Viking, 1 Bellevue Ave., Newport. Double room $79-$269. 401-847-3300.

Bed & Breakfast, Newport. 401-846-5408.

Bed & Breakfast Registry at Newport. 401-846-0362.

Newport Historic Inns, Newport. 401-846-7666.

White Horse Tavern, corner Marlborough and Farewell sts., Newport. Open for dinner nightly 6-9. $$$$. 401-849-3600.

Preservation Society of Newport. Schedules for admission to the mansions vary throughout the year, so call for information. 401-847-1000.

Franklin Spa, 229 Spring St., Newport. 401-847-3540.

Poor Richard's, 254 Thames St., Newport. Open daily 7-4:30. $. 401-846-8768.

Spirit of Newport, Treadway Inn Marina, Newport. Tickets $6. 401-849-3575.

Cookie Jar, Bowen's Wharf, Newport. Open daily 10-6. 401-846-5078.

Miniature Occasions and Dolls, 57 Bellevue Ave., Newport. Open Monday-Saturday 10-5, Sunday 1-5. 401-849-5440.

Armchair Sailor Bookstore, Lee's Wharf, Newport. Open Monday-Saturday 10-6, Sunday noon-5. 401-847-4252.

Animation Art Gallery, 213 Goddard Row, Brick Market Place, Newport. Open daily 10-6. 401-849-2577.

The Mooring, Sayer's Wharf, Newport. Open daily noon-9. $$-$$$$. 401-846-2260.

Muriel's, corner Spring and Touro sts., Newport. Open for breakfast Monday-Saturday 8-11:30, Sunday 9-3. 401-849-7780.

Touro Synagogue, 85 Touro St., Newport. Open (by guided tour only) Memorial Day-July 3 Monday-Friday 1-3, Sunday 11-3; July 4-Labor Day Sunday-Friday 10-4; Columbus Day-Memorial Day Monday-Friday at 2 P.M. by appointment, Sunday 1-3. 401-847-4794.

Newport Historical Society, 82 Touro St., Newport. Walking tour May-October Friday and Saturday at 10 A.M. Tickets $5. 401-846-0813.

Salas' Restaurant, 345 Thames St., Newport. Open for lunch in summer Friday and Saturday only 11-3. 401-846-8772.

Black Pearl's Outdoor Café, Bannister's Wharf, Newport. Open daily 11:30-5:30. $-$$$. 401-846-5264.

Day Trip: Best Ocean View in the Ocean State

ONE JUNE DAY, ANXIOUS FOR A TASTE OF SUMMER, MY daughter and I escaped to the Ocean State. Sara, who is eight years old, spends her days pretending to be a puppy or pony — anything that does not resemble a human. Her perfect day must include animals. So we headed south in search of creatures great and small. Rhode Island is kid-size, perfect for car-antsy children because you can get anywhere there in 30 minutes. Here I share with you the highlights of our day trip. It is guaranteed to satisfy the most spirited members of your family.

I packed a picnic and Sara, and we arrived at the **Roger Williams Park Zoo** in Providence when it opened. Within two minutes she gasped, "Mom, look!" Just ahead stood a mother zebra nursing her baby. Sara's face told me the visit could have ended here and she would have been satisfied. We saw graceful Masai giraffes munching tall trees with an unlikely backdrop of racing cars on Interstate 95. With elephants lumbering nearby, we learned that each year an adult elephant in the wild walks over 10,000 miles and eats 110,000 pounds of food. Farther down the path she pointed to a pair of antelope and slowly sounded out the words on the sign — "Bongos live deep in the African forest and are rarely seen," she read in a whisper of wonder.

The zoo's population numbers nearly 1,000 animals, with over 150 species on display. Surrounding the zoo are 400 acres of manicured landscape that includes a museum of natural history, a planetarium, greenhouses, a carousel, Rhode Island-themed miniature golf, and the Dalrymple Boathouse, where you can rent paddleboats and mini speedboats to tour the park's waterways. Though the park affords breezes, shade, and refreshments, we both wanted to head to the sea.

We hopped back on I-95 and took 195 east through Fall River (Massachusetts) to North Tiverton (Rhode Island). Within 30 minutes we pulled into the small, shaded parking lot of the **Emilie Ruecker Wildlife Refuge,** a 47-acre birdwatcher's Eden owned by the Audubon Society of Rhode Island. The easy trails make it a nice hike for kids, and at low tide the shallow marshland along the Sakonnet River is a sure bet for finding fiddler crabs. Remember the binoculars. Shorebirds — herons, egrets, and the majestic great egret with snow-white wispy feathers — feed in the shallows here. Everywhere we walked, I smelled the sweet scent of shadbushes filled with waxwings and cardinals.

We toted lunch and the old wool car blanket to the gravel cove that divides the Emilie Ruecker Wildlife Refuge from adjacent Jack's Island. This six-acre peninsula offers a remote and peaceful glimpse back to the time of the Pocasset Indians, who grew white corn, beans, and pumpkins on this lowland hundreds of years ago. I'm told children frequently find arrowheads when local farmers till the land in the spring. Along Seapowet Avenue you'll find a state management area with plenty of places to park your car (for free). As Sara and I strolled over a bridge across the Sakonnet River, two boys with nets straightened their hunched backs long enough to show off a big blue crab.

It was early afternoon. Our next stop was **Henseforth Farm,** just a couple of miles south in Adamsville, where Jan Hensel and Ben Gifford raise alpacas. At the driveway we were greeted by a group of curious mopped-topped males.

Sara squealed with pleasure. One look at the alpaca and you'll see that this could be the prototype for all Disney characters — big, soulful eyes and soft, shaggy fur. Ben showed Sara around the farm, introducing her to each of their 32 alpacas: Hummington (alpacas are said to hum), Arthur, Foster, Storm Cloud, and others. The alpacas rivaled Jan's breathtaking gardens. When she is not gardening or tending the herd, she can be found in her garage "spinnery," turning the fine alpaca fur into yarn for knitting and weaving.

Ben told us to stop at Gray's Ice Cream a mile down the road at the junction of routes 77 and 179. Gray's opened in 1922 and is one of a handful of independent ice cream makers in New England. This was just what we needed to revive us for the last stop on our animal journey. I drove back to Tiverton, where I picked up 138 and headed west through Portsmouth, Middletown, and Newport over the Newport Bridge to Jamestown.

This little island with three state parks, camping, and miles of undeveloped beach is perfect for families with small

---

WHAT THE LOCALS KNOW

THE LARGEST SELECTION OF NATURAL FIBERS IN NEW ENGLAND

Ben Gifford, who raises the alpacas at Henseforth Farm, told me not to miss his sister Louise Silverman's yarn shop in Tiverton. Knitters from across the country come to Sakonnet Purls to find skeins, hanks, and balls of every imaginable fiber and color. There's silky merino wool, alpaca, llama, mohair, blends, and machine-washable wools specially designed for babies. Also featured are lots of patterns, including Louise's own "Friendly Patterns for the Average Knitter," with easy instructions color coded according to size.

Sakonnet Purls, Rte. 77 south of the lights at Tiverton Four Corners. Open Tuesday-Saturday 10-5, Sunday noon-5. 401-624-9902. For a brochure of Louise's knitting patterns, send a self-addressed-stamped envelope to 3988 Main Rd., Tiverton, RI 02878.

children. We've come to visit **Watson Farm,** a Society for the Preservation of New England Antiquities property. An inconspicuous sign off North Road leads to 285 acres of pasture and fields with broad views of Narragansett Bay. The farm is open to the public only three days a week in the afternoons. We picked up a brochure for a self-guided tour.

The two-mile walk starts at the barnyard, where I had difficulty pulling Sara away from a basket of mewing kittens. Though I'd taken her to see the rare Arabian oryx, I suspected that her brightest memory of the day might be this little calico clutching her shirt. Up the hill a windmill pumps water from an 80-foot well into a 2,000-gallon tank for the livestock. Farm manager Don Minto joined us for a part of the tour and delighted Sara with a display of his well-trained border collies, who obediently responded to his "That'll do." He and his wife, Heather, have spent nearly 20 years here raising three daughters in a quiet, hardworking way, not unlike the five generations of Watsons who farmed the land from 1784 until Thomas Carr Watson Jr. bequeathed it to the SPNEA in 1979.

Sara patted two massive black Percherons, wandered through fields among cows and calves, and cooed at a group of new lambs. The appeal of Watson Farm is not just its rural splendor but that it is a real working farm that produces beef, lamb, and wool.

By dinnertime Sara and I had walked nearly ten miles. We were starved. The **East Ferry Market & Deli** overlooking the harbor on Jamestown was the answer. It offers all sorts of deli sandwiches, quiche, pasta, and baked goods, including giant cookies dotted with M&Ms. We took our feast and drove to the southern tip of the island to **Beavertail State Park.** I've driven all over New England, and I am certain there is no better picnic spot anywhere.

Just past the lighthouse (and museum and outdoor toilets), we parked in lot # 3. Sara quickly scrambled down a huge outcropping of rocks. On one side a couple sat taking in the best ocean view in the Ocean State, and on the other two men and a boy fished. The low tide revealed pools filled with periwinkles and mussels. Sara picked her way across slippery rocks. She reached for a teeny crab and waved it in the air proudly. In the evening light the huge sandstone boulders glowed. The seaweed was brilliant green. We stayed until it was almost dark. Homeward, we played an alphabet game naming all the creatures we'd seen, starting with alpaca. About 30 seconds after we got to zebra, Sara was sound asleep.

– Polly Bannister

Essentials

Roger Williams Park Zoo, 1000 Elmwood Ave., Providence. Open every day except Christmas; April-October weekdays 9-5, summer weekends and holidays 9-6; November-March 9-4. Adults $5, seniors and children $2.50, under 3 free. 401-785-3510.

Emilie Ruecker Wildlife Refuge, 137 Seapowet Ave., Tiverton. 401-624-2759. (Information also available from the Audubon Society of R.I., 12 Sanderson Rd., Smithfield, RI 02917. 401-9490-5454.)

Henseforth Farm, 460 East Rd., Adamsville. From Tiverton Four Corners go east on Rte. 179 (East Rd.), farm is 1 mile on right. Call ahead for an appointment: 401-624-4184.

Watson Farm, 455 North Rd. Jamestown. Open June 1-October 15 Tuesday, Thursday, Sunday 1-5. Adults $3, seniors $2.50, children 6-12 $1.50, under 6 free. 401-423-0005.

East Ferry Market & Deli, 47 Conanicus Ave., Jamestown. Open daily 6-5, weekends 6-6. 401-423-1592.

Beavertail State Park, Beavertail Rd., open dawn to dusk. Beavertail Lighthouse Museum open Memorial Day to mid-June weekends noon-3; mid-June to Labor Day daily 10-4. 401-423-3270.

Index

Fresh Pasta Company,
Northampton, MA, 181, 183
Friends and Company, Madison,
CT, 205, 208
Frog Hollow, Manchester, VT,
107, 111
Frog Hollow on the Marketplace,
Burlington, VT, 121, 127
Frogwater Café, Camden, ME,
34, 37

G

Garden Gables Inn, Lenox, MA,
174, 177
Isabella Stewart Gardner Museum,
Boston, MA, 152-153, 156
Gaslight Grill, Portsmouth, NH,
62, 66
Mildred Georges Antiques,
Chatham, MA, 168, 171
Wendell Gilley Museum of Bird
Carving, Southwest Harbor, ME,
46, 49, 50
Gourmet Deli Café, Manchester
Center, VT, 108, 111
Governor's Inn, Ludlow, VT,
117, 119
Grams & Pennyweights Antiques,
Putnam, CT, 210, 212
Grand Isle Fish Culture Station,
Grand Isle, VT, 122-123, 127
Grand Patisserie, New Milford, CT,
195, 200
Grass Roots Antiques, Woodbury,
CT, 199, 201
Gray's Grist Mill, Adamsville,
RI, 227
Green Mountain Club, Waterbury
Center, VT, 137, 142
Green Mountain Glove, Randolph,
VT, 114
Green Mountain National Forest
District Office, Manchester
Center, VT, 145, 148
Green Pond Fish'n Gear, East
Falmouth, MA, 162, 163
Greensboro Free Library,
Greensboro, VT, 133
Green Street Café, Northampton,
MA, 182-183, 184

Grindle Point Sailor's Memorial
Museum and Lighthouse,
Islesboro, ME, 34, 37
Griswold Inn, Essex, CT, 191, 192
Florence Griswold Museum, Old
Lyme, CT, 191, 192, 206, 208
Guided "Stagecoach" Rides,
Gorham, NH, 87, 89
Guilford Handcrafts Gallery,
Guilford, CT, 205, 207
Gulf of Maine, Brunswick, ME,
28, 29

H

Isaiah Hall B&B, Dennis, MA,
167, 171
Hammonasset Beach State Park,
Madison, CT, 189, 190, 205,
207-208
Hampshire House, Boston, MA,
154-155, 156
John Hancock Tower, Boston, MA,
153, 156
Hanover Inn, Hanover, NH, 79, 81
J. J. Hapgood General Store, Peru,
VT, 109-110, 112
Harding's Book Shop, Portland,
ME, 19, 22
Harpswell Inn, Freeport, ME,
24, 29
Harraseeket Inn, Freeport, ME,
24, 29
The Harvest, Pomfret, CT, 210, 213
Haven, Vinalhaven, ME, 33, 36
Hawk Inn and Mountain Resort,
Plymouth, VT, 117-118, 119
Haymarket Café, Northampton,
MA, 181, 183
Hayseed, Litchfield, CT, 196, 200
Henseforth Farm, Adamsville, RI,
241-242, 244
Herbert Hotel, Kingfield, ME, 40, 44
Heritage New Hampshire, Glen,
NH, 86, 88
Heritage Plantation, Sandwich,
MA, 166, 170
Hero's Welcome, North Hero, VT,
124, 128
Highland House, Tamworth, NH,
72, 74